Mennonite Idealism and Higher Education

Mennonite Idealism and Higher Education

The Story of the Fresno Pacific College Idea

Edited by Paul Toews

The Center for Mennonite Brethren Studies
Fresno, California

The Center for Mennonite Brethren Studies, Fresno, CA 93727
© 1995 by the Center for Mennonite Brethren Studies

Book design by Kevin Enns-Rempel, Center for Mennonite Brethren Studies

Cover design by Gail Enns, Fresno Pacific College Graphics

Printing by Creative Teaching Associates, Fresno, CA.

Cover photo: Fresno Pacific College Public Relations .

ISBN 1-877941-05-0

Contents

PART THREE
REVISIONS AND OUTWORKINGS
OF THE FRESNO PACIFIC COLLEGE IDEA

Foreword

Perhaps more so than at any previous time, Christian colleges are today focusing anew on their identities. Undoubtedly this self-examination is, in part, a defensive action to guard against the "slippery slope" towards secularism. Aware of the many colleges that gradually abandoned their Christian identities, despite ongoing nominal denominational relationships, colleges determined to remain Christian are reinforcing their definitive Christian commitments.

Defensive posturing is not the only nor the primary reason for new mission statements. More importantly, Christian liberal arts colleges are coming of age. They are achieving increasing excellence and visibility. They are becoming a significant force in American higher education. The renewed identity statements speak the language of confidence and optimism. Their tone suggests that a new era for the Christian college seems just before us.

Yet the questions remains for each college to answer: what definitional language is appropriate to us? An incarnational faith, Christianity is always communicated in specific people, words, and communities. Christianity is never only an abstracted set of beliefs. It is always the Word becoming flesh. Hence, Christianity is communicated through many different denominational, inter/non/para-denominational, and theological languages. Therefore "Christian" — and even "Evangelical" — embraces a great variety of connotations depending on the speaker and the hearer. Hence each college will carefully craft its unique Christian identity appropriate to its particular sense of mission.

In defining its identity each Christian college must address two frequently competing agendas. The one is essentially conservative, that is of maintaining and communicating the particular heritage of the college. Colleges are stewards of the past, they preserve both the shame and the glory of the past to inform the present and the future. Thus they are guardians of specificity, of the particularities of faithfulness which God has used and blessed. The second is more expansive, that is of including and embracing a variety of people and perspectives. Most Christian colleges move significantly beyond the confines of their denominational heritage. This is almost always a constructive and creative dynamic. It enriches the specific with the ecumenical. Balancing these two agendas is almost always a challenging imperative.

The Fresno Pacific College Idea is an unusually rich articulation of a Christian college identity. The 1995 version builds on a 1982 revision of the 1966 original. The original formulation influenced by the neo-Evangelicalism and neo-Anabaptism of the day, sought to move beyond a fundamentalist past to combine the best of the Mennonite Brethren heritage with the best of liberal arts education. The product of visionary young professors recruited by President Wiebe, the Idea evidenced a creative and bold vision, perhaps unmatched in its detail and breadth by any other Mennonite college.

The original Idea sought to carefully balance Mennonite Brethren specificity with evangelical ecumenicity. Yet it did not adequately address professional and graduate studies. And as increasing numbers of non-traditionally Mennonite Brethren students, faculty and administrators joined the Fresno Pacific community, the balance in the original some believed over-emphasized Mennonite specificity. Interestingly, Mennonite Brethren pastors encouraged the College to de-emphasize the tradition in favor of a more generic Evangelicalism. They were the liberalizers while faculty were the conservatives.

The 1995 Idea is a rebalancing and rearticulation of the original. While retaining most of the original essence, it speaks in languages more readily heard and understood today. It communicates the Fresno Pacific College identity to an increasingly pluralistic community. The neo-Anabaptism so evident in the original is not lost but its prophetic vision of the faithful church and the coming Kingdom is reformulated for a new generation and a new era. It is a statement of confidence and optimism for the future.

The Pacific College Idea will surely continue to serve Fresno Pacific College very well as it is increasingly recognized to be a leading Christian college on the West Coast. The Idea can also serve as a very helpful model for every other Christian college defining its own unique identity. The evolution of the Idea chronicled in the following pages will certainly prove instructive to colleges seeking to be faithful to their past and their present as they anticipate the future. This volume on Christian college identity is most timely and will be warmly welcomed as Christian colleges redefine their mission for these challenging and exciting days.

Rodney J. Sawatsky
President, Messiah College

Introduction

During the 1994-1995 academic year Fresno Pacific College is celebrating its fiftieth anniversary. In the history of American colleges, that is a short history. Yet fifty years is also an appropriate time to reflect on a college's story. This collection of essays is not, strictly speaking, a history of the college. Joel A. Wiebe already has written an institutionally sponsored history — *Remembering . . . Reaching: A Vision of Service* — for the fiftieth anniversary celebrations.[1] This slender volume has a more narrow focus. It seeks to describe the idealism that has shaped the college, particularly the liberal arts phase since 1960.

The opening in the fall of 1944 of Pacific Bible Institute — the precursor to Fresno Pacific College — was the fulfillment of a dream long held among Mennonite Brethren on the West Coast. Mennonite Brethren congregations were first established in California's San Joaquin Valley during the first decade of the twentieth century.[2] By 1916 the five MB congregations on the West Coast were already discussing the need for a school in California. In so doing, they expressed sentiments deeply embedded in the Mennonite Brethren imagination. The Mennonite Brethren commitment to the schooling of the next generation dates back to the origin of the denomination in 1860 in the Russian empire. Among the elements present in the formation of the new group was a yearning for greater educational and cultural freedom than was practiced within the authoritarian structure of the Mennonite colonies in Russia. A disproportionate number of young teachers eager to explore how Western European learning and culture might reinvigorate Russian Mennonite religious life were part of the initial Mennonite Brethren movement.[3]

The subsequent history of Russian Mennonite migration to North America, beginning in the 1870s, includes the establishment of schools almost as quickly as that of congregations. In 1908 the MB Church founded Tabor College in Hillsboro, Kansas, its own four-year liberal arts college.[4] In the West, the Reedley, California settlement was established in 1905, and by 1910 it began a winter Bible school program.

In 1922 a private educational society was established by interested Mennonite Brethren in the central San Joaquin area. Through the sale of $100 memberships they hoped to establish Bethany College in order to provide every young Mennonite Brethren with "a religious as well as a scientific education."[5] That project was finally realized in 1944.

The reasons for the delay are numerous. The intervening years witnessed political and economic stresses that alone were sufficient to delay such a venture: the trauma of being Germanic in two world wars, the economics of becoming established, coping with the Depression, and the absorption of countless new migrants from the Midwest. But the more serious reasons for the delay were theological.

The impulse to build a school was rooted in the need to insure that MB young people would receive appropriate denominational understandings. Denominational schools are typically nurseries of denominational piety. They shelter people from the corrosive impact of alien ways. But the question of what is to be mediated to the next generation can sometimes become unclear.

The 1920s to the 1940s was such a time of uncertainty for West Coast Mennonite Brethren. Some of them were drawn to American Fundamentalism, an aggressive and crusading movement to fight cultural and theological modernism. During the 1920s and 1930s, as the fundamentalist-modernist debate polarized American Protestantism, Mennonite Brethren instinctively leaned into the conservative camp. They did so without the slightest hint of theological modernism in their denomination. As an immigrant group still feeling like outsiders, they might have been put off by the Americanness of fundamentalism, yet in a world of simple dichotomies they stood with the fundamentalists. Other Mennonite Brethren found new freedom in the Pentecostal-Holiness movement that contrasted with their own restrained and codified piety.[6]

While a conservative theology emphasizing doctrinal certitude and expressive piety historically have been part of the Mennonite Brethren, they were now highlighted in some quarters as being more true and necessary than previously. As these interests gained ascendancy among those fostering the development of the new school, one observer reflected the theological differences present in the early 1940s: "many of our old standbys are not at all in sympathy with what these men are trying to feed us. . . . They constantly speak of having a school in which we instruct our young people in the ways and beliefs of our fathers, but if our fathers would arise from the dead and observe, I am sure they would not recognize some of our ways."[7]

This uncertainty about what kind of school and what kinds of theology would best nurture the Mennonite Brethren was not yet resolved when Pacific Bible Institute opened in 1944. It began very much in the tradition of the American Bible institute with objectives, program and character consonant with similar institutions across the country. To be sure, it also had some denominational distinctives, and it flourished during the first years. From a beginning enrollment of 28 students in 1944 it grew rapidly to 178 students by 1949. Then began a persistent decline that reached a low of 57 students in 1958. Clearly a different kind of institution and educational ideal was necessary to attract the support of West Coast Mennonite Brethren.

In the late 1950s Pacific Bible Institute began a metamorphosis that turned it into Fresno Pacific College, a liberal arts college. In 1956 the decision was made to add a junior college curriculum to the Bible institute program. By 1965 the college earned full accreditation as a baccalaureate institution and ten year later, in 1975, it was authorized to offer Master's degrees.

The decline of the Bible institute program and the necessity of moving toward a liberal arts institution created possibilities of many kinds. It was a time for asking fundamental questions. What kind of college should emerge? What kinds of philosophical, religious and educational ideals should shape the transformed institution? To answer those questions the institution's Board of Education, in 1960, hired Arthur Wiebe as the new President. Wiebe, together with a new faculty that he recruited, began the task of rethinking questions of institutional mission and identity. The result of their process of planning and inquiry would eventually be articulated as the "Fresno Pacific College Idea." That idea has since shaped much of the self-understanding and development of the college. It has been the lodestar that has guided many college decisions. Faculty in particular have been prone to ask how every new program matches with the idea statement. Invoking the idea has been a bit like calling up a sacred mantra that could either legitimate what at first glance seemed an unacceptable suggestion, or tarnish and even cast into oblivion established practices. The idea has been used both to protect and extend the institution's center and boundaries. Like the ideation that shaped the Pacific Bible Institute years, the "FPC Idea" has also had its critics and supporters. The debate about institutional identity and mission did not end with the formulation of the Idea statement. But the statement has been at the center of all subsequent discussions about the meaning of Fresno Pacific College.

The Fresno Pacific College Idea when it was first formulated in 1966 contained seven essential ideas:

Pacific College is a Christian College
Pacific College is a Community
Pacific College is a Liberal Arts College
Pacific College is an Experimental College
Pacific College is an Anabaptist-Mennonite College
Pacific College is a Non-Sectarian College
Pacific College is a Prophetic College

For all of the power that the idea has had in the life of the institution, it has never received a full explication. These essays seek to understand the factors producing the idea statement, offer extended explication of its central elements, and examine its continuing role in the life of the college. They offer not a chronological development of Fresno Pacific College, but are a perhaps more elusive attempt to understand the ferment of ideas and conviction that have been the ideational core of the college.

The history of institutional development is the layering of programs, of diversification, of programmatic enlargement. Amidst the growth and even fragmentation that accompanies most stories of institutional development is the attempt to maintain a synoptic vision. The tension in maintaining a distinctive core while serving ever more publics is not uncommon to Christian colleges. This quest for the distinctive and appropriate ideational core not only defines institutional mission but also energizes a school. While debates about core institutional ideas may seem arcane and even superfluous to the supporters and friends of a college, and sometimes even to trustees, they are necessary and critical for institutional survival. In fact, those Christian colleges that are most successful are probably those that have worked hardest at defining such an ideational core and then worked at juxtaposing and balancing it with the needs of the world around them.

These essays are part of the ongoing discussion about that balancing act. They are the singular interpretations of the authors. Unlike the Idea itself, these interpretations have not been canonized through the interminable process of dialogue that Mennonites sometimes call the "hermeneutics of community." For the most part they were written by people with long tenure at the college. With the exception of John Yoder, the authors have been associated with the college for at least twenty-five years. They reflect a history of concern, conviction and even leadership in defining Fresno Pacific's ideational core. They do reflect the love affair that many of us have with this little college, an affair rooted in the idealism of the "Fresno Pacific College Idea."

NOTES

1. Joel A. Wiebe, *Remembering . . . Reaching: A Vision of Service – A Fifty Year History of Fresno Pacific College* (Fresno Calif.: Fresno Pacific College, 1994).

2. See Kevin Enns-Rempel, "A New Life in the West: Settlement and Colonization on the Pacific Coast," in *75 Years of Fellowship: Pacific District Conference of the Mennonite Brethren Churches, 1912-1987*, ed. Esther Jost (Fresno Calif.: Pacific District Conference of Mennonite Brethren Churches, 1987), 9-23.

3. The historiography on the origins of the Mennonite Brethren in Russia is extensive. Selected important works include: Peter M. Friesen, *The Mennonite Brotherhood in Russia (1789-1910)*, trans. and ed. J. B. Toews, et al. (Fresno, Calif.: Board of Christian Literature, General Conference of Mennonite Brethren Churches, 1978); John A. Toews, *A History of the Mennonite Brethren Church: Pilgrim and Pioneers* (Fresno, Calif.: Board of Christian Literature, General Conference of Mennonite Brethren Churches, 1975); John B. Toews, *Perilous Journey: the Mennonite Brethren in Nineteenth Century Russia, 1860-1910* (Winnipeg: Kindred Press, 1988); James Urry, "The Social Background to the Emergence of the Mennonite Brethren in Nineteenth Century Russia," *Journal of Mennonite Studies* 6 (1988): 8-35; Paul Toews, "Differing Historical Imaginations and the Changing Identity of the Mennonite Brethren," in *Anabaptism Revisited: Essays on Anabaptist/Mennonite studies in honor of C. J. Dyck*, ed. Walter Klaassen (Scottdale, Pa.: Herald Press, 1992), 155-172.

4. For the history of Tabor see Wesley J. Prieb and Don Ratzlaff, *To a Higher Plane of Vision* (Hillsboro, Kans.: Tabor College, 1983); William Schmidt, "A History of Tabor College" (M.A. thesis, University of Wichita, 1961); Paul Toews, "Henry W. Lohrenz and Tabor College," *Mennonite Life* 38 (September 1983): 11-19.

5. See report in *Verhandlungen der dreizehnten Pacific Distrikt-Konferenz der M. B. Gemeinde, abgehalten vom 11. bis 14. November, 1922, zu Dallas, Oregon,* 22.

6. I have more fully explored some of these theological issues in "'A Shelter In a Time of Storm': The Establishment of Schools in the Pacific District," in *75 Years of Fellowship*, 57-70.

7. Robert C. Seibel to Henry W. Lohrenz, 3 July 1944, Henry W. Lohrenz Papers, Correspondence: R. C. Seibel, Center for Mennonite Brethren Studies, Fresno, Calif.

PART ONE

Background to the Fresno Pacific College Idea

Chapter 1

The Birth of the Vision

Arthur J. Wiebe

The story behind the events that transformed Pacific Bible Institute and Junior College in 1960 into Pacific College of Fresno as an accredited Christian liberal arts senior college in 1965 is both a personal and institutional one. The personal saga began during the 1959 Christmas season. Our family had returned to Reedley, California to spend the holidays with my parents and family. The visit provided a welcome break from doctoral studies at Stanford University. Little did we realize how events during this visit would impact our future.

During the week after Christmas, Peter A. Enns, a member of the Mennonite Brethren Board of Education, called to ask whether I would meet with the Board's West Area Committee for the purpose of discussing Pacific Bible Institute. Arrangements were made to meet with Enns and fellow members Menno S. Gaede and Peter Funk at Gaede's residence. We were all well acquainted because of my twelve years of previous service at Immanuel Academy, a Mennonite Brethren high school in Reedley.

"We would like to discuss the future of PBI with you," Enns stated at the outset. "You are familiar with the program and history of PBI over the years. We are trying to find out where we should go from here and would like to hear your suggestions. Our enrollment continues to decline and we soon need to make a decision about its future. Shall we close PBI, revise its direction, or continue to struggle along with the present program? What do you see as the future for Pacific Bible Institute?"

What surprised me most was that they even were discussing the possibility of closing Pacific Bible Institute. It quickly became clear, however, that these men were seriously considering all options.

I had some knowledge about PBI and its program from numerous visits there with senior classes of Immanuel and occasional discussions with faculty members. I quickly realized, however, that my limited knowledge provided an insufficient basis for making any thoughtful observations. After sharing this feeling of inadequacy with the board members, I suggested that they discuss their observations and concerns further to understand why all three alternatives were being considered. We devoted several hours to a wide-ranging, informative discussion of questions and issues surrounding the PBI's program that provided a better understanding of why the members considered the Institute to be at the crossroads.

Behind their concerns was the short but changing history of the Institute. Established in 1944, Pacific offered a typical three-year Bible institute program. Enrollment had grown steadily, peaking in 1949-1950 with 190 day school students. By that time PBI was evolving into a four-year Bible college offering B. A. and Th. B. degrees. The first baccalaureate degrees were conferred in 1953.

During this time there was a growing concern within the Mennonite Brethren Conference about the viability of supporting two four-year higher education institutions, Tabor College in Hillsboro, Kansas and PBI in Fresno. As a result, the 1954 conference made a historic decision to unify all Mennonite Brethren higher education programs within the United States. A newly-elected Board of Education was charged with the responsibility for designing and carrying out a unified program. After extensive and prayerful consideration the board developed a master plan that designated Tabor College as the conference's senior liberal arts college, proposed the establishment of a seminary, and reduced the role of PBI from that of a four-year Bible college to that of three-year Bible institute. The seminary was to be established in Fresno and affiliated with PBI. The two West Coast schools were placed under the administration of a single president. Further, the board decided that steps leading to the accreditation of Tabor College should be given high priority.

Understandably, this decision had a demoralizing impact on the administration and faculty of Pacific and its supporting constituency. During the December 1954 board sessions, President Rueben M. Baerg observed "the need for a stabilizing of our Bible Institute program." The urgency of the need was evident from the general unsettled feeling among students and faculty. The school had undergone a reversal in attendance — from 190 in 1950 to 80 in 1954. Furthermore the records of the past five years made it increasingly clear that demand for more liberal arts was rising. If, therefore, PBI could offer a more expanded program in liberal arts education, lower division work, and Bible institute, Baerg believed the "immediate urgency could be met rather satisfactorily."[1] The board responded positively and accepted the recommendation "that the program of the West include the development of the junior college."[2] The target date for this initiative was set for the fall of 1957.

Rueben Baerg resigned as president in 1954, at which time an administrative committee was established until a new president could be chosen. In a report to the board in May 1955 on behalf of that committee, faculty member G. W. Peters reported that "the attitude towards the Bible Institute is one of neutrality. It will take much and hard work to build up a Bible Institute complex." He anticipated no more than twelve to fifteen students in the Bible institute. Some students would return for the sacred music diploma, but the entire Bible institute program needed to be "sold to our constituency." Peters further reported that most students would be attracted to the liberal arts courses. In spite of this gloomy analysis, he reassured the board that the administration and faculty were determined to give their best efforts. "We have succeeded in pulling ourselves out of a spirit of depression. There is interest and enthusiasm. . . . Much hard work and tactful selling will have to be done to recapture the interest, sacrifice, and willingness of our churches and especially the students."[3]

Enrollment continued to decline, causing increased concern within the Board of Education. In his September 1956 report to the Board's West Coast Area Committee, newly-appointed President B. J. Braun recommended that "in order to captivate the interest of as many of our youth as possible for our own conference educational program," the Board of Education should immediately establish a junior college program consisting of sixty hours of liberal arts work and eight hours of Bible.[4] The board responded positively to Braun's recommendation by authorizing the inauguration of the junior college program in 1956. This move marked the first departure from the initial master plan that the Board of Education had articulated in 1954.

Meanwhile, in spite of many reasons for discouragement, the Board of Trustees of the Pacific District Conference of Mennonite Brethren Churches began searching for land in southeast Fresno on which to locate a new campus for the school. In 1955 the board purchased fifty-three acres, from which they withheld thirty-three acres for the development of a residential subdivision and church. The income from selling those lots would make possible a gift of twenty acres to PBI. Enough lots were sold to bring the project to a successful conclusion. Now PBI had the land for a campus, but there was no money to develop the newly-acquired property.

This lack of progress in campus development added to the feelings of discouragement. The 1954 master plan included the construction of facilities on both the Fresno and Hillsboro campuses. Two separate fund-raising programs were initiated, one to support operations and the second to fund capital improvements. Because regional accreditation of Tabor College was a high priority, the first construction project to be authorized was that of the Tabor College library. The second project was to be the construction of a classroom-administration facility on the new PBI campus. Both fund-raising efforts lagged and it became necessary to use all funds for operations. The campus improvement program ended with the construction of the Tabor College library.

In his May 1958 report to the West Coast Area Committee, President B. J. Braun expressed his frustration at these developments:

> Your president was greatly burdened by this state of affairs. He [clings] to the conviction that there is a need for such a school as P.B.I. in this vast San Joaquin Valley. If we fail and P.B.I. closes down, someone else will come and do the job. Furthermore, the brethren now on the Board and administration would never outlive the accusation that we had sold P.B.I. "down the river." The prophets of doom would triumph and the proponents of faith would have to hang their heads in shame.[5]

The board responded as best they could by approving the construction of a classroom building. It was to be financed largely by a loan against the existing downtown campus and constructed with as much volunteer labor as possible.

The new twenty-acre campus, construction of the classroom building and addition of the junior college liberal arts program, however, failed to stem the continuing decline in enrollment. By the fall of 1959, only sixty-four students were enrolled, with a full-time equivalency of fifty-eight students. The fact that forty-one were first year students underscored the problem of rapid student turnover.

With such experiences during the first five years of unification, it is small wonder that these members of the board were open to all options in our December 1959 meeting. At the close of the meeting P. A. Enns commented in parting, "If you have any further observations or suggestions, we would be happy to hear from you." I felt helpless and discouraged as I left the meeting. These friends of mine were so committed and cared so deeply about PBI and yet there was so little I could offer them.

The drive back to our home in Belmont, California began with sharing the joys of the Christmas season and our visit with the parental family. As our conversation lapsed into silence each of us turned to our private thoughts. My attention soon returned to the haunting question posed by the Board members. Stubbornly, the question persisted despite attempts to think of other things. Could it be that the noble work begun through PBI, sustained by the prayers and dedicated efforts of so many, would have to end? Such a defeat seemed so unthinkable. Surely, there must be a solution so this mission of the church could continue!

For many miles I thought about ways in which the Board could address the question of PBI's future. What was the full range of alternatives? Which were the most viable? What was the potential of each course of action? What information did we need for intelligent decision-making? What necessary information was available and what needed to be assembled? How should we procure the needed information?

It became increasingly apparent that a lack of appropriate information had made our meeting in Reedley inconclusive. Therefore, high priority would need to be assigned to assembling and analyzing the necessary information. But who should take the responsibility for conducting such a study?

While rounding a well-remembered bend in the highway just east of Gilroy, I was struck that a remarkable match existed between this need for information and my current studies in higher education at Stanford. The abundant resources of the university, its faculty in higher education, and the many visiting educational leaders would be readily accessible. Should I suggest to the board that they undertake a thorough study of alternate courses of action? Should I offer my services to conduct it? I wrestled with these questions for the remainder of the trip, finally concluding to share my thinking with these men.

That evening I called P. A. Enns to suggest such a study and to indicate my willingness to take responsibility for conducting it. He immediately expressed a strong interest in the suggestion but wanted first to consult with the other members of the West Area Committee before responding. Later that evening, he called and requested that I fly back to Fresno as soon as possible to discuss the matter further.

At the ensuing meeting the rationale for and scope of the proposed study was discussed at length. Board members agreed that it was essential to assemble all the information necessary for making a recommendation that would chart the future direction for PBI. They would give all options thoughtful consideration but would recommend only the one with greatest promise. By consensus the board agreed that I was in the best strategic position to conduct the study and make the recommendation.

During the return flight the magnitude of this new responsibility began to dawn on me. Any recommendation, if adopted, would significantly impact many lives and shape the future mission of an institution built through the dedicated efforts of so many faithful supporters. On the one hand I battled serious misgivings about having consented to undertake such a serious assignment; on the other, it was a stimulating and exciting challenge and I became eager to begin.

The weeks that followed were marked by intense activity. I consulted with officials in key agencies, including the regional accrediting association, the State Department of Education, local colleges, and higher education faculty. From these contacts emerged an external assessment of the viability of the alternatives. Communication with many junior college administrators provided alternatives for designing the liberal arts program. An in-depth study involving the churches in the Pacific District allowed us to calculate how many Mennonite Brethren students expected to graduate from high school for each of the next fifteen years. I consulted studies analyzing the choices Mennonite Brethren students were making in higher education, and explored the potential for attracting students from other evangelical churches. The possibility of attracting qualified Mennonite Brethren faculty members was given serious study.

I also analyzed the status of PBI and its program. The major obstacles Pacific faced became apparent. Neither of its programs was accredited, a matter of growing concern to students, administration and board. Faculty turnover was a very serious and continuing problem. Joel Wiebe, the dean, had resigned to complete his doctoral studies, leaving only two full-time faculty members—Dietrich Friesen and Donald Braun—committed to returning for the 1960 fall semester. The operation was divided among three locations: the library, dining hall, and women's residence were housed in the downtown building; the men's residence was at a second downtown location, and the classroom building was located on the new campus in southeast Fresno. Library and laboratory resources were woefully inadequate. The student body was small and lacked continuity. Few students remained for more than a year. Meager financial resources prevented timely completion of necessary campus improvements. The operating budget was minimal. The conference financing plan for constructing a building on the new campus collapsed after the library building at Tabor was completed. The conference master plan imposed severe restrictions, limiting options for action. The non-Mennonite public was largely uninformed about PBI's existence. Most troublesome was the lack of a clear sense of direction that negatively impacted faculty and student morale.

But there were positive factors as well. Dedicated board members were highly supportive of efforts to find ways to empower the institution in fulfilling its mission of Christian education. Time and again they displayed a willingness to take bold action in facing daunting challenges. The recent emergence of the junior college liberal arts program had sparked a slight increase in interest in the institution as evidenced by the enrollment of forty-one first year students in the fall of 1959. Their retention could form the base for enrollment growth in the following year. Acquisition of the new campus through the efforts of the Pacific District Conference and the construction of the first classroom building showed conference support and the board's determination to move ahead. The school was strategically located in a major metropolitan area. A population of nearly a million resided within a hundred miles of the campus. Pacific would be the only accredited Christian college in this region and thus would have the potential to draw many students.

The study reviewed all these factors, both positive and negative. While helpful, this information was not sufficient in itself to serve as the basis for charting the course for the future. The spirit and mission of the Mennonite Brethren Church, the historic factors that had led to the founding of PBI, and what it meant to be an Anabaptist-Mennonite college somehow had to be addressed as well.

How could all of this fit together? How could it be woven into a meaningful plan of action? Where was the lodestar to guide the task? The establishment of an ambitious international mission program and the founding of Tabor and PBI were ways in which Mennonite Brethren expressed obedience to the Great Commission of Jesus Christ. The future PBI had to fit into this picture.

By 1960 Mennonite Brethren were face to face with new challenges resulting from growing urbanization, increased interaction with the broader society, and a broadening participation in the professions. All of this called for a liberal arts education. Increased interest in advanced education was also evident in those third world countries where the church had missionary programs. It was imperative, therefore, that any expansion in the PBI mission and program meet these growing challenges. All of this led me to the conclusion that Pacific could best meet its objectives by offering a quality liberal arts higher education program based on Anabaptist-Mennonite principles.

All of the factors began to point in one direction: Pacific would have to become an accredited, Christian senior liberal arts college in the Anabaptist-Mennonite tradition with a strong biblical studies division at the center of its program. At that time it seemed reasonable to assume that a strengthened Bible institute program could survive only if included as one component of such a division.

But this option presented a serious problem: it was in sharp conflict with the conference higher education master plan! How would I dare propose it? If proposed as the guiding vision for the future, the conflict would have to be resolved at the outset since the move to becoming a senior college was the cornerstone for all of my other proposals. Despite this obstacle, I was determined to submit a proposal for institutional development based on the senior college option. After all, it was only a recommendation and the board could always reject it.

With this decision as a foundation, clarity emerged as to necessary first steps. Both the Bible institute and junior college curricula would have to be rethought and reshaped to align with this vision. In the belief that Christian institutions must be among the best, academic excellence would have to become the hallmark of Pacific's programs. The focus would shift to the training of leaders, requiring that student recruitment focus on attracting students with leadership potential. Committed and highly qualified liberal arts faculty members would need to be recruited and encouraged to give extended periods of service to the institution. Faculty salaries would have to be raised. The library collection and laboratories resources would need major expansion. Additional facilities would need construction. Financial support would have to be broadened to provide the funds required to achieve these objectives.

The first draft was ready for submission to the West Area Committee of the Board at its meeting in late January 1960. Attending this meeting were Ed J. Peters, Chairman of the unified board, and West Area Committee members P. A. Enns, M. S. Gaede, and Peter Funk. After reviewing the findings, I presented three recommendations.

First, the only viable long-term option for PBI was to become an accredited senior liberal arts college in the Anabaptist-Mennonite tradition with the Bible institute as one of its major programs. Therefore, at least the West Area Committee of the Board would have to support moving in this direction for any of the remaining recommendations to have meaning. For the move toward this long-term goal I outlined an incremental approach in which each successive step would be fully tested. The most important steps were to be accreditation of the junior college program, success in faculty recruitment, significant growth in enrollment, and demonstrated ability to construct and equip the needed facilities.

Second, immediate priority should be given to strengthening the three-year Bible institute program through expanded course offerings, augmented faculty, and an energetic, conference-wide student recruitment program as permitted under the master plan. During the 1950s administrators had frequently raised the question about whether a demand for the continuation of a Bible institute still existed. Implementation of this proposal would provide a thorough, good-faith test of the viability of the Bible institute program. If successful, these efforts would help recapture the support of Bible institute enthusiasts, increase enrollment, add continuity and maturity to the student body, and restore this program to its former level. If unsuccessful, it would show that there was insufficient interest within our conference to justify retaining the Bible institute program as such and require finding an acceptable alternative that would serve the same mission.

Third, the junior college liberal arts program should simultaneously be broadened and realigned with the typical lower division offerings of a senior college. Such strengthening of the curriculum should be accompanied by an intensive recruitment effort. In contrast to recruitment for the Bible institute, the Mennonite Brethren Pacific District Conference master plan restricted junior college recruitment primarily to the West Coast. Biblical studies would remain the central component of the liberal arts curriculum. Academic expectations in all areas would be raised and additional well-qualified liberal arts faculty recruited as soon as feasible.

The recommendation that Pacific should plan to become a senior liberal arts college at an appropriate time in the future engendered the liveliest discussion. Surprisingly, it seemed to find ready acceptance from all those present, though they must have been keenly aware of the difficulty such a move would face in obtaining conference approval. Fortunately, their extensive professional and business experience provided them with a necessary perspective on higher education to consider this recommendation.

In support of this, I presented a ten-year projection of the impact that implementation of these recommendations could have on annual enrollments. This projection was based on a careful analysis of the data and observations gathered during the study. In my mind it was realistic and achievable with energetic leadership. Nevertheless, it was optimistic to expect board members to view it with confidence given a history in which enrollment had not passed ninety students since 1954. Were they shocked, amused, trusting or disbelieving when I projected an enrollment of 350 full-time equivalent students for 1970? This represented a six-fold increase over the current enrollment and was twice the previous record enrollment!

Their reaction to the projection was not easy to read. However, their immediate reaction was that this was the kind of optimism and enthusiasm they had been waiting for. "We have said 'Giddap!' long enough," Peter Enns responded. "We want to be able to say 'Whoa!'"

How did my projections square with subsequent reality? The following table compares the 1960 projection with the actual enrollments as supplied by the registrar's office. Both are expressed in full-time equivalents. In retrospect, the projections were not optimistic enough! God prospered the college beyond our highest hopes! Instead of a six-fold increase, God blessed us abundantly by making it seven-fold. My report also targeted 1970 as the year in which the decision about becoming a senior college would have to be made assuming growth reached these projections. The move to senior college status actually took place in 1965.

Toward the end of the session, Chairman E. J. Peters turned to me and asked, "When are you coming to make it happen?" Taken by surprise, I paused for a considerable time to absorb the enormity of the question. I responded that I considered my task completed with the submission of the study and its recommendations. I was not prepared to consider any further involvement.

Projected vs. Actual Enrollment
at Pacific College:
1962-1971

Year	Projected FTE	Actual FTE
1962-63	100	153
1963-64	124	201
1964-65	145	212
1965-66	170	232
1966-67	190	233
1967-68	210	305
1968-69	240	329
1969-70	270	318
1970-71	350	406

But these board members were not readily deterred. During the discussion that followed they repeatedly urged that I consider assuming leadership for the implementation of the proposed program. With reluctance, I promised that Evelyn and I would give their invitation serious and prayerful consideration, looking for God's clear direction before responding. It was clear to me that a positive response would require making a long-term commitment to achieve the recommended objectives. It would also require a complete reorientation of our plans for the future, given the promising chance for an internship with the U. S. Office of Education sponsored by the Ford Foundation.

Making the decision preoccupied our thinking in the days that followed. Because of information uncovered by the study, it was easy to visualize the great potential for Pacific. Accepting the invitation would open a unique opportunity to develop an accredited senior Christian liberal arts college built on Anabaptist-Mennonite understandings in a populous region of the country served by no other Christian college.

On the other hand, the task would be daunting and require tremendous effort. So little of what was envisioned actually existed. Consensus would have to be developed before we could begin moving in the direction recommended. A faculty of high quality would have to be recruited. We would need to design and construct facilities. Economic challenges would need successful resolution. Prospective students would need to become convinced that Pacific could meet their needs, and much greater support from the constituency would have to be rallied. I became tired just thinking about the energy that would be required.

Finally it was the vision of a Christian senior liberal arts college expressing an Anabaptist-Mennonite understanding of Scripture and mission that led us to accept the board's invitation. However, agreement would have to be reached on several matters. Foremost among these was the need for the West Area Committee to affirm its commitment to the vision presented with the steps deemed necessary to transform it into reality. We arranged a meeting with the West Area Committee for mid-February 1960 to resolve these remaining questions.

The most significant matter needing agreement was my recommendation that "should the natural growth dictate, there will be no bar against having a senior college on the West Coast." This required that at least the West Area Committee immediately come to grips with this fundamental question. It will forever be a tribute to these men that they had the courage and foresight to pursue this goal even while recognizing that it would require a basic revision in the master plan. These men had a deep appreciation for the role of liberal arts education and also Bible institute training. Clearly they shared the conviction that Pacific as a Christian liberal arts college could greatly expand its mission and make a significant contribution to California's Central Valley and beyond. Their education and extensive experience in the professional and business worlds balanced by their strong allegiance to the church provided them with the required perspective for addressing the questions raised by the vision. Finally, these men had the requisite courage and resourcefulness, valuable assets for charting the new course.

A second decision had to do with administrative structure. In 1960, the seminary and PBI were under the administration of a single president. Day-to-day operations at Pacific were under the direction of its dean. The lack of clear role definitions for the president and dean often created duplication of effort, frustration and even embarrassing situations such as each scheduling a speaker for the same chapel. (In at least some instances they resolved this situation by giving both speakers an opportunity to speak, giving the greater time to the one coming from the greater distance). To provide for effective leadership, I requested that the administration be restructured so that Pacific would operate independently from the Seminary with the president of Pacific reporting directly to the board.

A third recommendation dealt with using the designation "Pacific College" in all literature to replace "Pacific Bible Institute and Junior College." The rationale was that it would more clearly and accurately describe the emerging program. While we recognized that deleting "Bible" from the name might create misunderstanding, we reasoned that the aggressive plan for interpreting the new vision would mitigate such negative reaction.

Finally, arrangements were made for me to complete my doctoral residence at Stanford before coming to the campus full-time. During the interim I took responsibility for institutional planning and implementation, while the dean handled day-to-day on-campus administration. Since Joel Wiebe had resigned as dean to resume his doctoral studies, the board appointed Theodore R. (T. R.) Nickel, a long time public school administrator, as the on-campus administrator. With agreement on these matters, I accepted the leadership position. During the February 20-23, 1960 meetings the full Board ratified my appointment and approved the administrative restructuring

Acceptance of this new assignment occasioned a personal re-examination of all the issues raised during the study. The challenge was now very personal and inescapable. While aggressive action was called for, each step of implementation would need to be taken with great deliberation. My central concern was that the "spirit and mission of the Mennonite Brethren" should guide program development. Such an understanding is always a deeply personal one. Therefore, I devoted many hours to clarifying this understanding while walking the streets around our home in Belmont. I asked myself many questions: What does it mean to be Mennonite Brethren and what is the mission of that church? Does Christian higher education fit into our idea of mission? What special contributions could Mennonite Brethren make to the larger society through Christian higher education? What spiritual and intellectual resources can we bring to bear on this mission?

My growing up "Mennonite Brethren" had been a positive experience that had shaped my understanding of our "spirit and mission." My father was a longtime pastor and evangelist deeply involved in conference programs. Our home in Corn, Oklahoma was the "motel" where visiting Mennonite Brethren leaders dined and lodged, much to my delight. Each visitor contributed in a unique way to building my understandings and values. Dinner time provided the setting for many interesting and instructive experiences. The humorous stories of Rev. Cornelius N. Hiebert, the "behind the scenes" information shared by missionaries, and the insightful interpretations of Scripture by Rev. Abraham H. Unruh reflected the range of these powerful influences. Four years as a student at Corn Bible Academy and another at Tabor College, a year of teaching at Corn Bible Academy and twelve at Immanuel Academy, extensive involvement in church activities, and a growing appreciation for our Anabaptist heritage developed during Civilian Public Service in the Second World War all contributed to my understanding of Mennonite Brethren identity. This perspective was broadened and enriched through the completion of degree programs at two public universities and a doctoral program in progress at Stanford. Assuming the leadership role would put the composite understanding gained through these experiences to the test.

We assigned first priority to the review and revision of the curriculum with the goal of building strong three-year Bible institute and two-year junior college programs. In the process we negotiated additional instructional time from seminary faculty to make possible an immediate expansion of the biblical studies offerings. After accepting appointment as campus administrator, T. R. Nickel was forced to resign for health reasons. Joel Wiebe consented to delay resuming his doctoral studies and accepted the on-site administrative role.

Because of the rapid changes being made, we decided not to print a catalog for the 1960-1961 academic year. Rather, we printed two brochures, one for interpreting the Bible institute and the other for the junior college. Students had to decide in which program to enroll.

The Bible institute brochure was mailed to every Mennonite Brethren family in the United States. It described the expanded Bible curriculum and augmented faculty. Students of all ages were encouraged to consider spending a year or two in Bible study at Pacific. Two open letters describing and promoting the Bible institute appeared in *The Christian Leader* to inform the constituency that this program was returning to its former breadth. Letters were sent to all Mennonite Brethren pastors in the United States urging them to promote the Bible institute. By policy, the junior college brochure mailing went out only to the west coast but included both Mennonite Brethren and non-Mennonite families.

In an effort to retain as many students as possible, particularly the forty-one first year students, we immediately informed them about the developing program and plans for the future. We tried to identify other denominational groups that would welcome recruitment among their students. Service to the larger Christian community was an important component of our mission. In recruiting potential young faculty members I frequently articulated that ecumenical aspiration by suggesting that "Pacific College can be a significant education center for the Christian young people of many evangelical denominations."

We immediately consulted with Dr. Mitchell Briggs, Secretary of the Western College Association, regarding steps necessary for regional junior college accreditation. For several years Dr. Briggs had been urging the administration of PBI to seek accreditation. He believed it was the only way that Pacific had a future. He was very responsive to our expression of intent and immediately scheduled a preliminary visit. Because of this visit, the regional accrediting agency approved a full-scale visit for the fall of 1960.

We were advised it would not be necessary to prepare the normal self-study since their primary attention would focus on our plans for institutional development. Nonetheless, Joel Wiebe and I decided to complete the normal full self study. We submitted it to the regional accreditation commission in May 1960.

Because of a favorable recommendation from the visiting team, Pacific received junior college accreditation in early 1961. Pacific College thus became the first Mennonite Brethren institution to receive regional accreditation and the first Christian junior college ever accredited by the Western Association of Schools and Colleges (WASC).

Simultaneously, we gave serious attention to building the faculty. The college was fortunate in that it could draw upon the seminary faculty for instruction in biblical studies. The development and implementation of a long-range strategy for recruitment was imperative, however, particularly for the liberal arts faculty. Our immediate strategy was to aggressively recruit young Mennonite Brethren scholars emerging from graduate schools. In March 1960 I wrote enthusiastically to Dalton Reimer, a young MB student completing a Master's degree at Northwestern University, that "I am interested in tapping the top young men of our conference for this program. . . . With the experience and maturity of the seminary faculty and the enthusiasm, recent training, and scholarly minds available in the young men being added, we should have an unbeatable combination." Reimer became the first such young scholar to join our faculty in the fall of 1960. He immediately inaugurated a strong speech curriculum that served both the institute and college programs well.

Within three years, Reimer was followed in quick succession by Gary Nachtigall, Peter Klassen, Daniel Isaak, John E. Toews, and Larry Warkentin, all young scholars. Elias Wiebe's appointment as academic dean in 1962 added maturity and experience. By 1966, Harold Enns, Wilfred Martens, John Redekop, Jonathan Knaupp and Wilbert Reimer had joined the faculty. In retrospect, the decade of the 1960s was unique in the number of young scholars with an Anabaptist-Mennonite orientation emerging from graduate schools eager to join the Pacific College faculty.

Also important was the length of tenure that these young faculty members would give to Pacific College. The previous experience with frequent faculty turnover had made the board cautious in their expectations regarding tenure. Given the high quality of the emerging faculty, the board cautioned the administration to be satisfied if these scholars gave five years of service to Pacific. Half of those on the faculty in 1966, however, still serve today or did so until their retirement. Many of the others gave extended service. This stability provided a firm foundation for institutional development.

Recognizing that Pacific College could provide a quality experience for young men wishing to fulfill their national obligation through government-recognized voluntary service instead of military service, we aggressively sought Selective Service System approval for the establishment of an alternative service unit. Representatives of the Mennonite Central Committee were most helpful in helping us to obtain approval of such a unit in the spring of 1960. Within weeks, Robert Klassen entered our unit as college librarian. He brought excellent credentials, holding a graduate degree in library science, and had valuable experience as a librarian in the California State Library. His coming was most fortunate. Having made a sharp upward revision of the library acquisitions budget we needed Klassen's experience and expertise in making selections, supervising processing and screening out books no longer of value. After screening was completed only about six thousand remained. The rapid growth resulting from new acquisitions strained all available resources but Klassen never compromised the excellence of his work.

How should the library be housed on the new campus? The lone building on the twenty acres had classrooms and offices only. Improvisation was the order of the day. Two classrooms were set aside to serve as the "library." Somehow, Robert Klassen made it function in that severely limited space. But that was soon to change.

A fortunate development occurred early in 1961. I received a call from P. A. Enns, who was attending the board meetings in Hillsboro, Kansas. He informed me that Cornelius and Elizabeth Hiebert of Los Angeles were willing to fund the construction and furnishing of a library with a gift annuity, replicating the Tabor College library. Enns asked, "Would you favor accepting the offer and could the budget be revised to include the annual annuity payments?" Without waiting a moment, I responded with a resounding "Yes!" We could always worry about how to revise the budget later.

Two significant forces were now complementing each other: rapid book acquisition and the construction of a beautiful, spacious and highly functional library. The new library became an outward symbol of Pacific's move into a new and brighter future. In 1965 the tragic demise of Upland College in southern California led to the acquisition of its library holdings in exchange for our assuming custodial responsibility of its academic records. With this acquisition, the Pacific College collection doubled to forty thousand volumes almost overnight. Processing this addition was a monumental task, accomplished under the leadership of librarian Adonijah Pauls.

Would the constituency accept the new vision for Pacific College? To obtain the answer we conducted a series of presentations in Mennonite Brethren churches and at the Pacific District Conference to interpret the vision for the institution's future and its underlying rationale. We included four themes in each presentation.

I emphasized that broadening the nature of Pacific's program represented a legitimate expansion of our historic commitment to missions. As a denomination we had sent missionaries to the far corners of the world. Through Pacific College we now had the opportunity to minister to those in the San Joaquin Valley in a similar manner.

As the college would grow in recognition, our character as Mennonite Brethren would be tested. More ecumenical relationships would require us to constantly engage in self-examination about whether we were representing the Christian faith at its best.

To accomplish its mission, Pacific College would have to earn the respect of the public for its academic excellence and spiritual vitality. Too often, Christian schools and institutions are associated with mediocrity. Pacific could not afford to be so identified. Our reputation must be above reproach. Therefore, high academic standards must become a hallmark of the institution.

Pacific College was shifting its emphasis to leadership training for all walks of life. Therefore, its program would progressively be expanded to offer sound and relevant training to a broader spectrum of students.

The reception to this interpretation of the vision was generally positive. A few constituents expressed concern that the emphasis on high standards of scholarship would overshadow the Christian mission of the college. The great majority, however, recognized that a college of excellence would serve both the church and the larger society. Mennonite Brethren laypersons, in particular, evidenced a remarkable understanding of the need for Pacific to develop as a liberal arts institution and rallied to give the vision strong affirmation. Many seemed energized by the new developments. But we also received words of caution amid the encouragement. "Remember that PBI represents the sweat and blood of many of us," A. A. Schroeter, one of the founders of the institution, admonished, "Don't forsake the purpose for which it was founded!" He voiced the concern of many that we stay true to the institution's original purpose even while recognizing that the new approach was necessary to effectively serve our mission and the changing needs of Mennonite Brethren youth.

An experience in November 1960 significantly fortified my resolve to make a long-term commitment to Pacific. The Shafter Mennonite Brethren Church invited me to give the afternoon address during their fall harvest thanksgiving festival. My parents accompanied Evelyn and me on this occasion. During the trip down my father and I engaged in an extensive and memorable discussion of challenges facing the Mennonite Brethren just as we had on many previous occasions. He encouraged me to render my best in the mission to which I had committed myself. I was already keenly aware of his prayerful support.

We shared the noon meal with several of our many friends in the Shafter congregation. My father had been their interim pastor for several years. Following lunch I went to the car to meditate in preparation for the message. Shortly, someone rushed to tell me that my father was very ill. I found him in the church's anteroom in excruciating pain. He had suffered a massive heart attack. Recognizing his end was near he spoke longingly that "I would like to stay with the family longer." With the final words, "God's grace is sufficient even for this hour," he left us to go to his reward.

It was a difficult choice to remain and make the presentation but I knew my father would have encouraged me to do so. Graciously,

Pastor Henry H. Dick offered to release me but I felt compelled to stay. Within the hour it was time to interpret the vision for Pacific to an understanding audience. I felt as though I was doubly commissioned, first by our heavenly father and now by my earthly father. Afterwards, Board Chairman E. J. Peters comforted and reminded us that, "This is what it is all about!" We needed to focus all of the educational efforts of Pacific College on eternal values and our eternal destiny.

The college prospered. In the fall of 1960 enrollment increased by more than 40 percent to ninety-two students. Despite the emphasis we had given to strengthening and promoting the Bible institute program, enrollment in it dropped in the fall of 1960 to just eighteen students. Simultaneously, enrollment in the junior college program nearly doubled to seventy-four students.

The Bible institute option had been given a final full and fair test with discouraging results that seemed to confirm the observations made by previous presidents during the 1950s. Clearly, it was time to reexamine how the founding purposes of PBI could be incorporated into an alternate approach. We chose a two-fold approach. The 1962-1964 college catalog promoted new three-year programs in Bible, Christian education, and church music to provide training in preparation for a life of service in the church.We also sought to embody the founding purposes in an academically strong liberal arts biblical studies program staffed by full-time faculty members to supplement part-time instructors from the seminary. In 1962 John E. Toews, a graduate of the seminary and subsequent long-term dean there, became the college's first full-time Biblical studies instructor.

By the spring of 1962 we felt institutional progress was so promising that initiation of the senior college program needed serious consideration. This was five years earlier than initially projected. So, while we were busy preparing the self-study for the next scheduled re-accreditation visit in the fall, we were also discussing the steps necessary for inaugurating a senior college program. During the WASC team visit we freely expressed our opinion that their next visit would likely be to evaluate Pacific as a senior college. Pacific's junior college accreditation was extended by WASC for three years. Stimulated by the self-study discussions, our faculty and administration immediately began to plan for the upper division majors in areas where faculty strength warranted.

More and more often we expressed our enthusiasm to the West Area Committee for adding the senior college program. Its members soon became part of the process, sharing our conviction that it was time to move toward this major and significant objective. Chairman E. J. Peters, M. S. Gaede, and P. A. Enns were key players in moving the agenda forward. By the fall of 1962 the full board began to discuss this question. Some expressed serious reservations while others were convinced it was the only alternative. Slowly, a consensus began to emerge. By summer they agreed to submit the question to the conference scheduled to convene in Mountain Lake, Minnesota in August 1963.

Meanwhile, sophomores who would be juniors in fall were facing a critical decision. Would the conference approve Pacific becoming a senior college? Should they risk enrolling in upper division courses knowing that the senior college program was not yet accredited?

The board members were aware that the recommendation for Pacific to become a senior college required a major departure from the 1954 master plan and that it would not meet with universal approval. After all, the objective of accreditation for Tabor College, a key reason for the structure of the master plan, had not yet been realized. Approval also meant that the conference would have two as-yet unaccredited senior colleges. In spite of all of this, the board moved ahead. Chairman E. J. Peters, a man of widely recognized stature among constituents promised, "I will lead this charge!" He played a key leadership role in interpreting the reasons for this move to the assembled delegates. Dr. Roy Just, President of Tabor, volunteered to make the motion to accept the board's recommendation, believing that doing so would help to rally support among Tabor alumni.

Elias Wiebe, the newly appointed dean of academic affairs, and I represented Pacific College in describing the opportunities that would result from becoming the only Christian senior liberal arts college in the San Joaquin Valley. Considerable discussion followed from the conference delegates. In the end, the conference approved the recommendation. Immediately, Elias and I located the nearest telephone to inform the faculty that we were now a senior college. Their reaction was electrifying! Our vision could now expand as a senior college.

That fall most of the juniors decided to stay, trusting that the senior college would be accredited by the time they graduated. With their enrollment, the senior college was underway. Faculty members frequently took on extra assignments to provide the needed courses and engage in institutional planning. Enrollment continued to increase making it possible to recruit additional faculty.

Senior college accreditation now became the primary objective. We launched a vigorous program to recruit additional faculty, develop and refine majors, expand library and laboratory resources, and recruit students. Growth in program and enrollment, in turn, placed continuous demand for additional facilities. As a result we broke ground for new buildings eight times in the 1960s. Each time we had to depend on God's provision and the faithful support of our constituency to solve the financial demands this placed on the institution.

Parallel to program development, the faculty and administration engaged in intensive discussions to define the nature of the college. These discussions were the seeds that sprouted into a formal statement known by the mid-1960s as the "Pacific College Idea." The story of that process is treated elsewhere in this volume.

To explore accreditation for the senior college, Elias Wiebe and I met with the secretary of WASC. He warned us that it was extremely risky to seek accreditation before our senior college graduates had validated our program by establishing a record of successful work in graduate schools. We said we couldn't wait and were prepared to accept the risks of an earlier visit. Hearing of this risk, the board nevertheless approved moving ahead immediately. The faculty were more than prepared to take the risk. We applied to WASC for a visit during 1964-1965, the first year we would have seniors. WASC scheduled its visit for early in 1965. With dedicated commitment, the faculty and administration, under the leadership of Elias Wiebe, worked feverishly to strengthen the senior college program and complete the self-study. Finally, all was ready for the WASC visit.

A major factor favoring us was the record we had established since being accredited as a junior college. We had responded positively and fully to each of the previous WASC recommendations and were developing as projected. Our self-study included an open and frank discussion of additional deficiencies. We admitted that these would need to be resolved quickly and outlined our plans for doing so. Yet we knew that these preparations did not remove the risk associated with an early attempt to secure accreditation.

At WASC's request, Elias Wiebe and I attended their meeting in Los Angeles on May 10, 1965, during which they would be reviewing the visiting team's report and making their decision. They wanted us in attendance to respond to further questions. Meanwhile the faculty had secretly made plans to celebrate in the event that Pacific received accreditation.

The plan was for Elias and me to call as soon as we knew whether we had received accreditation. If that occurred, everyone would spring into action carrying out predetermined assignments. Since some hours would elapse before we could fly back, they would have time to invite West Coast board members, local pastors, and other interested parties to the campus for a celebration upon our return.

The faculty arranged to have the student body, the board and the faculty to greet us at the airport. They had arranged for a white convertible to carry several board members, Elias and me in leading the parade back to campus.

At the meeting, WASC officials reviewed some of their concerns and asked for our plans to respond. Our hopes began to rise as the tone of the discussion became increasingly positive. They dismissed us so they could complete their decision making. A few minutes later they informed us of their decision.

Just a scant three weeks before our first seniors were to graduate, we were informed that WASC had granted Pacific College senior college accreditation! Hearts in our throats, we bade the officials a hurried good-bye and searched for the nearest telephone. A quick call to campus informed the faculty of the good news. They immediately sprang into action, informing students of this momentous development. All classes were canceled to begin the celebration.

The thoroughness of planning became apparent as we landed at the airport. Newspaper reporters and television crews were prepared for our arrival. Headed by Chairman E. J. Peters, the board members stepped onto the tarmac to congratulate us as representatives of the college as students and faculty cheered.

After a few comments reporting on our experience with the members of WASC, all headed for the cars to begin the parade. It was a jubilant crowd that paraded back to campus. It must be remembered that the mid-1960s were characterized by many marches protesting this and that. On the evening news one television reporter commented, "Today there was another student march in Fresno. But this one was different. The students of Pacific College marched in celebration of having been accorded senior college accreditation." The comment was doubly significant. It brought attention to Pacific's accreditation but also told the audience that there was something different about this college and its students.

We had reached another milestone! Building on this new foundation, Pacific College was poised to serve the mission of the church in an even larger way. The vision of 1960 had become the reality of 1965.

The road between will forever be marked by many acts of faith. Members of the board, members of the faculty, members of the student body, and many members of the Mennonite Brethren Church had combined their efforts to make the seemingly impossible happen. God added His blessing by honoring these many acts of faith. Accreditation of the senior college program opened up a new era, and brought added responsibility for using this new status to better serve the mission of the church.

NOTES

1. Minutes of the Annual Meeting of the Board of Education of the General Conference of the Mennonite Brethren Church of North America, 13-14 December 1954, Records of the Board of Education, Center for Mennonite Brethren Studies, Fresno, Calif. (Hereafter Board of Education Records).

2. Ibid.

3. "Report of the Administrative Committee of Pacific Bible Institute of Fresno, submitted to the Committee of the Board of Education, May 5, 1955," Minutes of the Meeting of the Board of Education of the General Conference of the Mennonite Brethren Church of North America, May 10-12, 1955, Board of Education Records.

4. Meeting of West Coast Area Committee of the General Conference Board of Education, September 15, 1956, Board of Education Records.

5. "Outline of the president's proposal made to the West Coast Area Committee on May 12, 1958," Board of Education Records.

Chapter 2

The Origins of the
Fresno Pacific College Idea

Dalton Reimer

The 1964-1965 academic year began the third decade of Pacific College's existence. The year was climaxed by senior college accreditation and the graduation of Pacific's first senior college class. The transition from Bible institute to senior liberal arts college begun toward the beginning of the school's second decade was now complete. At this point the focus of the college shifted to issues of longer-term direction. What kind of college should Pacific become? This question motivated an intense period of master planning, which in its early stages led to the formation of the "Pacific College Idea."

THE IDEA OF AN IDEA

"Idea" has been the favored word chosen by a variety of authors to signify a vision for a human activity. In higher education one might think of John Henry Newman's seminal nineteenth-century work, *The Idea of a University*,[1] or more recently Elton Trueblood's *The Idea of a College*,[2] or Arthur F. Holmes' *The Idea of a Christian College*.[3]

"The Pacific College Idea," originally written in 1966 and revised in 1982 and 1994, stands in this tradition. It is the vision for this particular college.

The Idea of an institution is really a coherent mix of ideas. It is a statement that reveals the center of an institution's identity, reason for existence, core values, view of communal order, and relationship to the world. Furthermore, an Idea is less a statement of present reality than a vision of the ideal. As such, it serves as a guide for the future, providing an anchor against aimless drift, a hedge against the fads of the moment. It is a dream of what might be, and so motivates continuing development and growth.

Institutions of learning need centers. Warren Bryan Martin, then a Research Educator at the Center for Research and Development in Higher Education at the University of California, observed in the mid-1960s:

> There are not many colleges in America, and almost no state universities, characterized by values so distinctive as to really shape the life of the place. The value vacuum at the institutional center and the near anarchy with regard to norms and models everywhere else . . . leave the student either with no definite standard against which to test himself or with only the value presuppositions of various departments — unexamined within many departments and often conflicting among departments — out of which to devise some sort of total configurational awareness. The result is an identity crisis for the institution and a disintegrative learning experience for the student.
>
> American universities have encouraged the exploration of ideological alternatives in the classroom. We know how to keep a lot of balls in the air at the same time. But the personal commitments of the faculties and administrators have seemed so malleable or so minimal that students have often concluded that a hierarchy of values is unnecessary or impossible. But a life without distinctions is boring, even as one without meaning is death. Men cannot live in a value vacuum any more than they can live in an oxygen vacuum.[4]

An institutional Idea, then, not only provides the center that is essential to the continuing renewal of life within the institution. It also enables the institution to most effectively realize its primary mission of teaching and learning.

In 1966, a few months after graduating its first senior class, the Pacific College faculty and administration embarked on a quest to form an Idea that would guide the further development of this young college. This quest was motivated by a deep concern that the college be shaped not only through an adaptive response to the external needs of its environment and constituency, but most significantly by a center that reflected the core beliefs and values of its particular traditions. Though the results of the quest came to be called the "Idea," it was not a Platonic or philosophical quest. Rather, it was a quest deeply rooted in the recognition that communities are fundamentally shaped by their "stories." So the formers of the Idea returned to their key stories—the Christian story, the Anabaptist-Mennonite story, and the story of the Liberal Arts. They sought to articulate in the Idea a vision that integrated coherently the wisdom of these traditions from the perspective of Christ centeredness.

TRANSFORMATIONS IN THE FRESNO PACIFIC VISION

The Pacific College Idea of the mid-1960s was the culmination of several transformations in the vision of this changing school. Earlier visions can be deduced from statements of purpose and other related statements appearing generally in the Bible institute and early college catalogs. These serve as background to the formation of the Idea during the mid-1960s, and help to illuminate the continuities and discontinuities in the history of the institution.

The institution, since its beginning in 1944 as the Pacific Bible Institute, has consistently represented itself as a Christian and as a Mennonite Brethren-sponsored institution. Though church-related, it has also from the beginning represented itself as a non-sectarian institution embracing persons from various Christian traditions. The 1945-1946 bulletin, for example, contains the following statement:

> The Pacific Bible Institute is a denominational school of the Mennonite Brethren Conference of the Pacific Coast District. The school as such, however, is not sectarian in its program of instruction, but it "earnestly contends for the faith which was once delivered unto the saints." If there are doctrinal points in which our denomination differs from other groups of Believers, we do not in any way enforce our views upon them, but prayerfully seek the guidance of the Holy Spirit as we examine the views in the light of the Scriptures.
>
> We love Christian fellowship and extend a warm welcome to all students of other denominations who adhere to the fundamental doctrines of the Christian faith, and are zealous in the promotion

of His Cause. Instruction is free (a small registration fee is charged of all students) to students of any denomination. [5]

The statement reflects the traditional Anabaptist-Mennonite understanding of faith as a voluntary rather than forced commitment. It also affirms the Scriptures as the authoritative guide to faith while opening the door to seeking truth together. It also invites like-minded persons into Christian fellowship across denominational boundaries. A form of this statement was included in subsequent annual catalogs of the institute. Later, a specific section on the non-sectarian nature of the college appeared in the Pacific College Idea.

With the transformation of Pacific Bible Institute into a liberal arts college, a deliberate decision was made to be not only non-sectarian, but to open the doors of the college even further to non-Christians. All students who wished to pursue an education in a Christian college, who met the academic requirements of the college and who were willing to commit themselves to the requirements of the community were welcome. This admission policy was viewed as consistent with the churches' mission of both evangelizing and discipling.

Educationally, the institution has moved through several transformations. It began as a Bible institute, evolving during the 1950s into a Bible institute/Bible college and then a Bible institute/junior college. In the early 1960s it was transformed to a junior college and later a senior college, and by the mid-1970s included graduate and professional education programs. In brief, these changes are mirrored in the statements of purpose put forward in the institute and college catalogs. The purposes and character of the original institute are suggested in the school's initial bulletin (1944) under the title "The Aims of the School":

1. To uphold a positive interpretation of the Scriptures.
2. To strive constantly to maintain a spiritual atmosphere which will tend to lead students into a fully consecrated life.
3. To develop a sincere love for mankind and an intense desire for their salvation.
4. To help each student acquire a skill in practical Christian work through a supervised program of personal work.
5. To uphold the principles of peace, separation from the world, simplicity of life, sanctity of the home, and diligent habits of industry.
6. To train and equip students for pastors, evangelists, S.S. workers, missionaries and personal soul winners.

The second year a seventh aim was added:

7. To instruct men and women in Christian thought, life and service and to hold in high regard the sacredness of the family institution.

These seven aims are repeated in each year's catalog through the 1949-1950 academic year. They represent evangelical Christian values and also the particular emphases on such matters as "peace, separation from the world, simplicity of life, sanctity of the home, and diligent habits of industry" that have been part of the larger Anabaptist-Mennonite understanding of faith. Vocationally, they represent a Bible institute's narrower agenda of preparing workers for the church.

In 1950 several changes occurred. The seven earlier aims were reduced to five under the title of "Purpose of the School in General Terms":

1. To give young people a thorough knowledge of the Bible, the Word of God.
2. To train them in the highest type of Christian living in whatever walk of life they may find themselves.
3. To prepare them for Christian service, in the homeland or mission fields abroad.
4. To fortify them against the various unscriptural philosophies of life.
5. To send forth sanctified Christ-like personalities, yielded and obedient to the Master.

This list is restated in each subsequent catalog through 1955-1956. As a more general summary of the earlier list of seven, this reformulated list deletes specific references to such historic emphases in the Mennonite tradition as "the principles of peace, separation from the world, simplicity of life," and others identified particularly in the fifth aim of the earlier list. The fourth purpose in the new list — "To fortify them against the various unscriptural philosophies of life" — introduced for the first time a defensive tone into the statement of purposes.

The revised statement was amended with the addition of a two-year liberal arts curriculum in 1956-1957. The first purpose was revised as follows: "To give young people a thorough knowledge of the Bible, the Word of God, *and a Bible based world and life view*" (added words in italics). In 1957-1958 the fifth purpose was deleted.

The 1950s, in summary, represented a more generalized and yet narrower vision as judged from these public statements of purpose and curricular changes. The original purposes were reworked into more general statements, particular historic Anabaptist-Mennonite values such as peace were no longer specifically referenced,[6] and a fortification purpose was introduced as a defense "against the various unscriptural philosophies of life." These changes, together with the consistent decline in enrollment from a high of 190 students in the day program in 1949-1950 to a low of sixty-four in 1959-1960, suggest that by the end of the 1950s the institute was in both an identity and adaptive crisis.

The revisions of the statement of purposes in some ways paralleled a larger ideological narrowing that occurred in the country during the 1950s. It was the era of McCarthyism and the Cold War. The United States itself became a nation seeking to fortify itself against the larger evils of the world.

The 1960s, however, began on a different political note. Tapping into a reservoir of latent American idealism, President John F. Kennedy brought his 1961 inaugural address to a rousing climax with a strong challenge to the nation: "And so, my fellow Americans, ask not what your country can do for you: Ask what you can do for your country." The foremost concrete expression of this idealism was the Peace Corps. When the idea of the Peace Corps was first put forward by Kennedy at the University of Michigan during a campaign stop in the fall of 1960, Richard N. Goodwin, one of Kennedy's assistants at the time, reported that "seven hundred students . . . signed up for service in the nonexistent agency" within the first two days.[7]

At Pacific College, a new idealism also was taking hold in 1960. This was a year of major transition in the life of the institution. In February of 1960 Arthur J. Wiebe became Director of the Institute and Junior College. In March Wiebe introduced a series of new initiatives to the Board, including the renaming of Pacific Bible Institute and Junior College to Pacific College. Other actions followed. As a result, enrollment increased in the fall of 1960 by roughly 40 percent and continued to increase in subsequent years. After a decade of declining enrollments, a new direction was established.

Change came quickly in the early 1960s. With movement toward a senior college program a new statement of purposes for the college was needed. On December 2, 1963 the faculty adopted a new statement proposed by faculty members Peter J. Klassen, Dalton Reimer and John E. Toews. This statement reflected the culmination of the progressive transformation of the institution from a Bible institute to a senior Christian liberal arts college:

> Pacific College is a church-related college of the arts and sciences. As a Christian college it encourages a personal commitment to Christ which is expressed in a life of discipleship. Believing in a basic unity of all truth, Pacific College is committed to the meaningful pursuit of truth in the various areas of knowledge and experience.
>
> It is therefore the purpose of Pacific College:
> 1. To give the student an understanding and appreciation of the principal areas of human knowledge and of the arts and a sense of the proper place of these disciplines in the universe of knowledge.
> 2. To help the student form a system of spiritual, intellectual, social, and aesthetic values consistent with basic principles of historic Christianity.
> 3. To foster a vital concern for the religious and secular communities and encourage meaningful participation in these communities.
> 4. To assist the student in realistic self evaluation and the development of mature attitudes toward others.
> 5. To encourage the development of creative thinking, thoughtful investigation, and critical evaluation.
> 6. To train the student to communicate effectively.
> 7. To equip the student with adequate undergraduate training for his chosen area of service.

This statement was the immediate precursor to the Pacific College Idea. In reaffirming "a personal commitment to Christ which is expressed in a life of discipleship," it followed the basic declaration of Christian faith as understood in the Anabaptist-Mennonite tradition. The final statement of the preamble asserted the "basic unity of all truth" and so established the base for the larger agenda of a Christian liberal arts college. The seven purpose statements then expressed an integration of central Christian values with the expansive agenda of a liberal arts education.

MASTER PLANNING THE FUTURE OF THE COLLEGE

At the beginning of its life as a four-year college in the mid-1960s, the administration and faculty joined in a collaborative, comprehensive master planning process to define the future of the college. It was a moment of opportunity. Having navigated a series of transitions and having successfully acquired senior college accreditation, attention now shifted to the longer-term future of the place. What kind of college should this become?

Creating a master plan for the future of the college was the immediate motivation for the development of the Idea. Conversation about academic master planning had begun in the Academic Committee in the fall of 1965. On February 2, 1966 the Academic Committee formally established a Master Planning Committee with the appointment of John Redekop (social sciences), Dalton Reimer (humanities), and John E. Toews (Biblical studies) as its members. Arthur J. Wiebe as President, Elias Wiebe as Dean of the Faculty, and Vernon Janzen as Dean of Students were ex-officio members of the Committee. Arthur J. Wiebe (administration) and Toews (faculty) were appointed as Co-Chairs.

In its first meeting on February 15, 1966, the new committee formed three subcommittees: a subcommittee on philosophy and objectives with Toews and Reimer as members, a subcommittee on programs with Redekop and Elias Wiebe as members, and a subcommittee on organization with Arthur Wiebe and Janzen as members.

With this structure in place the work of Master Planning the future of the college began. The summer of 1966 was a particularly intensive time for work. Co-chairs Wiebe and Toews attended a summer conference on academic planning sponsored by the Council for the Advancement of Small Colleges (CASC). The subcommittee on philosophy and objectives led in formulating what during the process became the Pacific College Idea. John E. Toews served as the principal writer. At the end of the summer, on August 31 and September 2, an intensive workshop of the Master Planning Committee occurred. Several subcommittee reports were reviewed during these days, including a draft of the Idea. The Committee resolved to forward some of these reports to the faculty, including a revised Pacific College Idea. At the Faculty Workshop of September 8, 1966, the Pacific College Idea was first introduced to the faculty.

The master planning process itself was carefully defined from the beginning. Nine "working principles" for master planning were articulated. The first of these placed responsibility for this planning centrally in the community itself: "It is fundamentally assumed that the development and implementation of the college master-plan is the responsibility of the *entire faculty*" [italics in original]. The second principle announced freedom for "individual faculty members, faculty committees, board members, or other individuals invited" to "initiate proposals or statements." Then "as each part of the plan is finalized by the committee it will be presented to the faculty and to the members of the board of education for evaluation, and to the student council as it seems appropriate."

The working principles recognized the importance of individual initiative, but also the ultimate primacy of the community. Independent thinking was important. Rodin's sculpture of a single seated man, bent over with elbow on knee and chin resting on hand, with gaze downward in deep thought, captures well the hope of the Master Planning Committee for significant independent thinking and reflection. But interdependent thinking was ultimately intensive, rigorous and determinative. Interdependent thinking entailed community, and community has been a central tenet of the Fresno Pacific Idea since its inception. Community did not negate independent thinking, but placed independent thinking in dialogue with other thinking. The community became the arena for testing, shaping and refining ideas. Some ideas merited discarding, others enhancing. The hermeneutic of community is one of "unfolding" rather than "imposing," to use Martin Buber's image. In the end, communities that participate in creating an idea will more likely own the idea.

To call attention to the importance of the community in forming the Idea is not insignificant. Institutions originate and change in different ways. They are sometimes the creation of single, strong leaders. But the way of the Anabaptist Mennonite tradition is to create through community. This did not negate the importance of strong leadership. President Arthur J. Wiebe was such a leader. Rather, it reflected an ideological commitment to a particular way of creating in which the President together with others still led, but the community was involved in a partnership that allowed for the full exercise of giftedness within the community.

THE COLLEGE COMMUNITY OF THE MID-1960s

A college is in reality several primary sub-communities, including students, faculty, staff, administration, and board of trustees. Each sub-community is important and contributes in unique ways to the life of a college. In the larger history of the institute and college, the vision, dedication and commitment of the early boards and leaders was exemplary. The forward looking and innovative disposition of the unified Mennonite Brethren Board of Education that came into being in 1954 was particularly critical in making the developments of the 1960s possible.

But the administration and faculty of the mid-1960s assumed special responsibility for leading in master planning and creating the Pacific College Idea. Sixteen fulltime faculty and teaching administrators are listed in the 1965-1966 college catalog, the academic year that master planning officially began. Of these only two had joined the faculty before 1960. Essentially a new faculty had been built since the transition in 1960.

This faculty consisted of bright, young Mennonite Brethren who had pursued undergraduate studies in both the institutions of the church and secular colleges and universities. They had pursued graduate studies in seminary and major American universities. They were intellectually equipped to pursue other opportunities, but they chose to return to their Mennonite Brethren roots. Except for the President and the Academic Dean, all had earned their bachelor degrees during the 1950s and early 1960s. In age they were mostly in their late twenties and early thirties. They were generally fresh out of seminary or university master's or doctoral programs.

While loyal to the Mennonite Brethren Church that had nurtured them, they were also in contact with other worlds. Key leaders among the faculty had connected along the way with this century's renaissance of Anabaptist studies. For them the theological roots of the Mennonite Brethren were found in the larger Mennonite and Anabaptist tradition. For some, Harold S. Bender's summative mid-century statement of "The Anabaptist Vision" became a kind of confession. Albert Keim, contemporary Mennonite historian, has called Bender's statement, originally the 1943 presidential address to the American Society of Church History, "the most influential Mennonite speech of the 20th century."[8] Bender set forth three core truths as the essence of the Anabaptist vision: "First, a new conception of the essence of Christianity as discipleship; second, a new conception of the church as a brotherhood; and third, a new ethic of love and nonresistance."[9]

The "Anabaptist vision" took hold at the college during the early 1960s. With the coming of Peter J. Klassen in 1962, with a Ph.D. in Reformation-Anabaptist history, the course in Mennonite History (as distinguished from the narrower Mennonite Brethren History) was re-introduced into the curriculum. Persons from the larger Mennonite community spoke in college chapels. The Mennonite Graduate Fellowship under the leadership of John E. Toews met on campus. During the intensive period of master planning itself from

1966-1968, Albert J. Meyer, a resourceful expert and guide in Mennonite higher education, was brought to campus for consultation.

But faculty members were also in contact with worlds beyond the larger Mennonite world. They were schooled in their particular disciplines and in touch with their appropriate disciplinary professional communities. College membership and active participation in the Council for the Advancement of Small Colleges (CASC) brought faculty and administrators in contact with small colleges across America, as well as resource persons in American higher education. Participation in the Federal Government's Title III Developing Institutions program beginning in the mid-1960s created yet another set of contacts. Through frequent accreditation visits in the 1960s the college also benefited from the insights of visiting team members and leaders in the Western Association of Schools and Colleges.

While connected to multiple worlds and eager to learn from these worlds, there was nevertheless a strong spirit of nonconformity and independence. Trends and currents in American higher education received intensive scrutiny, but in the end the focus was on growing a college that would contribute to the larger good by bearing witness to the distinctive tradition in which it was rooted. Little interest existed in growing another generic Christian college. The faculty sought to insure that Pacific College as a Mennonite Brethren institution would remain faithful to its particular theological heritage. The spirit was analogous to that of the founders of the Mennonite Brethren Church itself just over a century before. While charting a new course as a renewal movement in nineteenth century Russia, the founders made it clear that they were still children of Menno Simons and so were intent on pursuing a faith rooted in a serious commitment to following Jesus in all of life.

THE SHAPE OF THE IDEA

The original Idea of 1966 was organized in seven sections. Each section captured a key characteristic of the college:

Pacific College is a Christian College
Pacific College is a Community
Pacific College is a Liberal Arts College
Pacific College is an Experimental College
Pacific College is an Anabaptist-Mennonite College
Pacific College is a Non-Sectarian College
Pacific College is a Prophetic College

Three sections speak particularly to the identity of the college, its reason for existence, and its core values. These sections locate the college at the confluence of three major streams of history: Christian, Anabaptist-Mennonite, and Liberal Arts. As a post-classical institution it is a liberal arts college; as a post-Judaic institution it is a Christian college; as a post-Reformation institution it is an Anabaptist-Mennonite college. The historical conversation among these traditions has shaped the interpretive center of the institution.

The vision for community growing out of the confluence of the Christian, Anabaptist-Mennonite and Liberal Arts streams of history is articulated in the section on community. The college's self-understanding of its relationship to the world is expressed in the three remaining sections: non-sectarian, prophetic, and experimental.

The sections of the Idea are not mutually exclusive. They overlap and interact with each other. Together they form a picture of the whole. They portray the character of the college.

The self-understanding of the Idea itself is expressed in the opening and closing sentences:

"Pacific College is a deliberate and continuous attempt to realize a certain idea through theory and experience." (opening sentence)

"The Pacific idea is only a partially realized idea. But it is the idea that gives Pacific reason for existence, courage for growth, and stimulus for adventure." (closing sentences)

Thus, the assumption of the Idea was that the college will deliberately and intentionally become the particular place envisioned in the Idea. It will never perfectly realize the Idea, but the Idea provides the compass that points the direction.

A BRIEF HISTORY OF THE IDEA

The intensive period of master planning that produced the Pacific College Idea began in February of 1966 and ended at the conclusion of the 1967-1968 academic year. At that time John E. Toews, who had co-chaired the master planning process with President Wiebe, returned to graduate school for further studies. John Redekop, a member of the Programs Subcommittee, left to teach in his native Canada. Master planning continued, but now in a lower key. The Pacific College Idea, meanwhile, took on a life of its own. It appeared for the first time in the college catalog for 1969-1970, though in a truncated version. In 1972 the Idea took its place at the center of the college catalog in its full version. It has appeared in every college catalog since.

In 1973 the visiting accreditation team from the Western Association of Schools and Colleges, chaired by John Cantelon, then Academic Vice President of the University of Southern California, began their final report on the college as follows:

> Pacific College constitutes a small but vital example of genuine pluralism in American higher education. Because of its size but more because of the dedication of its faculty and administration, the institution has been successful in incarnating significant elements of what it terms "the Pacific Idea" throughout the academic life of the College. The ideals of the Mennonite Brethren are alive and well at Pacific.[10]

The team concluded their report with a strong affirmation of the Idea: "The evaluators also share a strong feeling that the Pacific Ideal is something of unique value which should be preserved and nourished in the American educational scene."[11]

Others apparently agreed with the accreditation team's assessment. At about the same time, *Christianity Today* found the Idea of sufficient larger interest to feature the college in an article entitled, "Creative Learning—'The Pacific College Idea.'"[12]

In 1982, and again in 1994, the Idea was revised. In this way, the Idea has taken on a life of its own. It has served as the institutional center, an anchor for the college. It has sparked innumerable conversations, stimulated debate, served as a base for questioning, and otherwise enlivened the community. The Idea remains the vision against which both present realities and future possibilities are tested, and provides the motivation for continued growth and development.

WILL THE CENTER HOLD?

The origin of an idea is one story. The future of an idea is another. Thus, the key question is: Will the center hold? Centers have a way of not holding with the passage of time. As William Butler Yeats poignantly observed in his poem, "The Second Coming": "Things fall apart; the center cannot hold."

It is a truth well known that the center did not hold for America's first colleges. The first mottoes of Harvard, "*Christo et Ecclesiae*" and

"*In Christi Gloriam*," are hardly descriptive of today's Harvard. Ideological anarchy may be closer to the truth. But Harvard is not alone. At the outset of the decade that produced the Pacific College Idea, Yale historian Sydney Alhstrom observed that a "major fact about American higher education is that, regardless of other shifting attitudes and practices, it has for three centuries been continually, remorselessly secularized." He went on to describe his view of the status of the church college in America at the time:

> In the vast majority of cases its existence [as a church college] is nominal rather than real. Only in a relatively few Church bodies is its vitality a matter of primary concern. And if by "Church college" we mean an institution which has its intellectual life devotedly rooted in the "apostolic succession" of Christian learning and which has a connection with the Church that is living, active, and strong, we may go still further to say that it has become a rarity.[13]

Ideas rarely exist in isolation. They exist in a marketplace where alternative visions compete for attention. This is true of the idea of a church college. In the same year that the Pacific College Idea was written, the Danforth Foundation published its comprehensive study of *Church-Sponsored Higher Education in the United States*.[14] This study was based on extensive data collected from church colleges across the country. Four types of church colleges emerged from the data: 1) the "defender of the faith college," characterized by a narrow purpose of preparing persons for leadership ("lay or clerical") in a particular church group with faculty, administration and students being mostly members of that group; 2) the "non-affirming college," characterized as a secularized college with diminished concern for faith issues and a loose relationship to the sponsoring church; 3) the "free Christian college," characterized as a faith affirming college that sees faith as a matter of informed and voluntary choice and seeks to create a dynamic mix of "academic excellence and religious vitality"; and 4) the "church-related university," characterized as an urban institution exhibiting multiple characteristics of diversity. Within this marketplace of church colleges, the creators of the Pacific College Idea envisioned a faith-affirming college resembling the Danforth Foundation's third option.

Choosing to be a faith affirming college, however, is not sufficient in itself. The religious marketplace offer many varieties of faith. No single understanding of Christian faith exists. One inevitably must choose. The options have been labeled in different ways: fundamentalism, conservatism, evangelicalism, neo-orthodoxy, liberalism, civil religion, the social gospel, the health and wealth gospel, to name but a few. The creators of the Idea chose to avoid the customary labels. Rather, they chose to remember their own particular spiritual parents, who had been labeled as "Anabaptists," meaning rebaptizers. This label stuck, but its surface meaning masked a deeper understanding of faith. For the Anabaptists, the Christian life was an intentional commitment to seek the Kingdom of God as modeled and taught by Jesus, without regard for compromises proposed by civil or religious authorities.

The choice to be a faith-affirming college in the Anabaptist tradition did not win universal endorsement in the sponsoring church in the 1960s, nor has it now. For some in the church, memory of their own faith tradition has faded. Newcomers have often not learned the story, and thus have no memory at all. For others, alternative options within the religious marketplace have simply been more attractive. Some have shied away from this understanding of faith because they perceive that it does not sell well in the marketplace. But here it is that the creators of the original Idea boldly centered the college. And others too have caught the vision.

Will this center hold? While history is not encouraging, a college that clearly articulates its center and continues actively to nurture this center in its thought and life will more likely remain true to its historic mission. To reframe an old saying, ironically once offered by a retired general: Ideas don't die, they just fade away. They rarely suffer dramatic deaths. More often they die from neglect and drift. Though the destiny of the original Idea in the life of the college has not always been certain, the fact that the Idea remains and has retained its essence through two revisions bears witness to its ongoing importance for Fresno Pacific College.

NOTES

1. *The Idea of a University Defined and Illustrated*: I. In Nine Discourses Delivered to the Catholics of Dublin [1852]; II. In Occasional Lectures and Essays Addressed to the Members of the Catholic University [1858]. Edited with introduction and notes by I. T. Ker (Oxford: Clarendon, 1976).

2. (New York: Harper, 1959).

3. (Grand Rapids, Mich.: Eerdmans, 1987).

4. Warren Bryan Martin, "Stalkers of Meaning," *Journal of Higher Education* 38 (1967): 363-373.

5. Pacific Bible Institute Catalog: 1945-1946, 8.

6. It is interesting to note that the course in Mennonite History (as distinguished from a narrower Mennonite Brethren History) was dropped from the curriculum at about this same time, further evidence that the institute was departing somewhat from its historical theological moorings.

7. Richard N. Goodwin, *Remembering America* (Boston: Little, Brown and Co., 1988), 120.

8. Albert N. Keim, "50 Years of the Anabaptist Vision," *Mennonite Weekly Review*, 5 May 1994, 1, 6.

9. Harold S. Bender, "The Anabaptist Vision," *Mennonite Quarterly Review* 28 (1944): 78.

10. John E. Cantelon, et al., "Report on the visit to Pacific College: Fresno, California, February 12-14, 1973, 1, Fresno Pacific College Academic Vice President Records, Center for Mennonite Brethren Studies, Fresno, Calif.

11. Ibid., 7.

12. 14 September 1973, 48-49.

13. Sydney Alhstrom, "Toward the Idea of a Church College," *The Christian Scholar* 43 (1960): 28,31.

14. Manning M. Patillo Jr. and Donald M. Mackenzie, *Church-Sponsored Higher Education in the United States* (Washington, D.C.: American Council on Education, 1966). See chapter 12: "Patterns of Institutional Character," 191-197.

PART TWO

Components of the
Fresno Pacific College Idea

Chapter 3

The "Christian College" As Heresy

Delbert Wiens

A MEDITATION ON THE "FALL"

The proverbs of Solomon, son of David, king of Israel:

> That men may know wisdom and instruction, understand
>   words of insight,
> receive instruction in wise dealing, righteousness, justice, and
>   equity;
> that prudence may be given to the simple, knowledge and
>   discretion to the youth —
> the wise man also may hear and increase in learning, and the
>   man of understanding acquire skill,
> to understand a proverb and a figure, the words of the wise
>   and their riddles.
> The fear of the Lord is the beginning of knowledge; fools
>   despise wisdom and instruction. (Proverbs 1:1-7, RSV)

Priests, prophets, and sages were the teachers in ancient Israel. Christian colleges also try to be priestly, and they sometimes claim to be prophetic. As institutions, however, they most nearly fit into the wisdom tradition. Therefore, it is appropriate to begin with the writings of the biblical sages.

But what has the fear of the Lord to do with "crying out for insight . . . [and seeking] it like silver?" "For the Lord gives wisdom;

from his mouth come knowledge and understanding." This is Proverbs 2:6, and it also is linked by the preceding verse to understanding the fear of the Lord. It is a good thing to seek knowledge and wisdom. Even the skeptical Preacher agreed. "Then I saw that wisdom excels folly as light excels darkness." Wisdom "makes [one's] face shine," "helps one to succeed," and "is better than might." Granted. But all such claims are surrounded by doubt that one can find it and that, if found, it amounts to much more than "a striving after wind. For in much wisdom is much vexation, and he who increases knowledge increases sorrow." After all, "much study is a weariness of the flesh." But the conclusion remains: "Fear God, and keep his commandments." (Ecclesiastes 2: 13; 8:1; 10:10; 9: 16; 1:17-18; 12:12-13.) Our warrant for seeking knowledge and understanding is real. It is also disquieting. It is good. It is also doubtful and dangerous. But at least we have an opening to think about our educational mission.

The wisdom teachers of Israel provided a meditation on this paradox in the story of Adam and Eve in the Garden of Eden. It is a story that has a great deal to say about Christian colleges and those of us who presume to teach in them. In that story the serpent stands for the teaching power of our world. The serpent was more subtle than any other wild creature that the Lord God had made. He said to the woman, "Did God say, 'You shall not eat of any tree of the garden?'" (Genesis 3:1)

The serpent is not Satan. At least, not yet. Nor does *wild* connote the savage and undisciplined. This is Eden, after all. The serpent is an astute teacher subtly guiding student Eve to think about her situation. This animal is astonishingly clever, no doubt, but the question is appropriate even for the innocent. To eat is to assimilate. What may and what may not be eaten? This is all quite natural and quite important, though economy and mythic verisimilitude expresses it better through the invention of the serpent.

The question is pedagogically sound. To convince yourself of this, ask it of someone and demand a "yes or "no" answer. A heuristic confusion necessarily follows, as Brevard Childs argued in his Old Testament course at Yale Divinity School. "Yes" implied that God may have demanded that the fruit of all trees be avoided. "No" implied that there was no prohibition at all. The shape of the question required a thoughtful explanation.

For the first time, Eve was forced to think *about* God, as Childs also pointed out. She became the first theologian!

And the woman said to the serpent. "We may eat of the fruit of the trees of the garden; but God said, You shall not eat of the fruit of the tree which is in the midst of the garden, neither shall you touch it, lest you die.'" (Genesis 3:2-3)

The last clause reveals her new state of mind. God had not told Adam that he could not touch it (2:16-17). Eve added that. The question had opened an abyss beneath her feet. Until now she had walked and worked and conversed in innocence with God and with her mate. She had lived physically and spiritually within the garden. Now she had to step outside it. Instead of interacting directly with God and Adam and the creatures, she had to think about what God had said and about her relation to that part of her environment. In her sudden anxiety, she strengthened the prohibition. She pushed the prohibited object even farther away, showing that she had accepted the possibility of eating its fruit. Now that God had become an object of thought and God's prohibition had become a datum to be pondered, a space for the very human freedom to think and to choose had been opened up. She had lost her innocence. Eve had not yet sinned, but now she had better think very hard indeed.

But the serpent said to the woman, "You will not die. For God knows that when you eat of it your eyes will be opened, and you will be like God, knowing good and evil." So when the woman saw that the tree was good for food, and that it was a delight to the eyes, and that the tree was to be desired to make one wise, she took of its fruit and ate; and she also gave some to her husband, and he ate. (3:4-6)

The sages who shaped this story must have known that Eve did not need the serpent's encouragement to take and eat. There were compelling enough reasons to draw near the tree. For one, she was not accustomed to unanswered questions. She had had no opportunity to grow accustomed to anxiety. Having lost the security of the unquestioned verities of the garden, she needed the certainty that could come from impersonal "truth." Had she been willing to live with doubt, she would not have sinned, at least not yet. But she had not yet had occasion to learn to live in trust that God would answer troubling questions at the right times. And so there was unaccustomed pressure to do something to resolve the anxiety.

There was an even better reason to eat. She needed what the tree had to offer in order to know whether or not she should eat of the tree. This was the tree of the knowledge of good and evil. its fruit was the ability to discern, to be wise (see 2 Sam. 14:17), even, presumably, to be moral. That was what she did not yet have, and was precisely what she now desperately needed.

The question alone was enough to drive Eve to eat. To eat of this tree was to become like God, or at least like the gods who made up the heavenly court. To eat was to learn how to discern truth from falsehood, wisdom from foolishness, good from evil, as God admitted in verse 22. To live with such power was not simply a "Fall." It was also a wonderful leap upward. In a single moment she would become a higher sort of human. At least in part she would become divine. And she was told that she would not die. "So when the woman saw that the tree was good for food, and that it was a delight to the eyes, and that the tree was to be desired to make one wise, she took of its fruit and ate; and she also gave some to her husband, and he ate." (3:6-7)

Eve saw this. There is little irony now. It is simply so. The fruit of this tree is physically, aesthetically, and intellectually good. None of us can wish to return to Eden. Even the power to frame a rational judgment that we should like to do so is the result of the very act that drove our parents and us from that primitive innocence. Every opening chapel in every Christian college campus should include a liturgy of thanks to the serpent for the gift we have received. But that liturgy must also include the next verses:

> Then the eyes of both were opened and they knew that they were naked; and they sewed fig leaves together and made themselves aprons. And they heard the sound of the Lord God walking in the garden in the cool of the day, and the man and his wife hid themselves from the presence of the Lord God among the trees of the garden. But the Lord God called to the man, and said to him, "Where are you?" And he said, "I heard the sound of thee in the garden, and I was afraid, because I was naked; and I hid myself." He said, "Who told you that you were naked? Have you eaten of the tree of which I commanded you not to eat?" (3:7-11)

Had the serpent lied? It would be as appropriate to ask whether God had. In 2:17 God had told Adam that the same day he ate of the tree he would die. The serpent denied that and, so far, he seemed to have gotten it right. But it is certain that that is not how the sages want us to understand the text. As the quotation from Proverbs 1 notes, the wise speak in proverbs and figures and riddles. Perhaps neither has lied. Nor has either told the whole truth. The serpent's truth is that eating this fruit is not in itself the cause of physical death (see verses 19 and 22-24).

God's truthfulness is saved by the recognition that there is more than one kind of death. Something did happen immediately. So drastic a kind of dying ensued that God in judgment and mercy insured that Adam and Eve—and we—would not have to live forever in the new condition, however ambiguously wonderful and elevating it was and continues to be. How are we to understand this?

The clue comes from two powerful "figures": eating and naked-ness. Knowledge and thinking, in one of their modes, imply both violence and alienation against both the subject matter and oneself. To eat this fruit Eve had to yank it from the tree. Perhaps even a bit of branch came with it. To eat the fruit she had to tear it apart and crush it, destroying it to gain its virtues. The quest for understand-ing, in one of its modes, is as aggressive and destructive as eating. By an act of the will the self detaches itself from its living, concrete environment (the all-grown-togetherness of a greater organism within which one responds as a thou to thous) and constitutes itself as a knowing subject over against some aspect of the former whole from which it is detached. Having become an object, it is now re-duced to a mere "it" for the sake of analysis, which itself is a process of "undressing" and of dissecting in order to examine the parts of which it is composed. This aspect of the dialectic of knowing is a form of killing. In the humanities, one analyzes the patterns, the strategies, and the devices of the composition chosen for analysis. During the length of that exercise, at least, one destroys the compo-sition as a whole and exchanges enjoyment of it for the always somewhat vicious pleasure of critiquing it. In the social sciences, one performs the same operations on oneself and one's societies. In the life sciences, one literally kills the "specimen" to dismember it. The advanced quest for knowledge always involves separation and alienation. Thinking kills. It does so even when its intention is the appreciation and preservation of life.

Unfortunately, learners become what they do. Having eaten, Adam and Eve turn their new powers upon themselves. For the first time they cease simply to be themselves for each other and before God. Each of them now becomes a knowing subject that turns upon itself, seeing themselves and each other as "mere" objects. "Then the eyes of both were opened and they knew that they were naked." Having "undressed," they sewed fig leaves to make aprons for themselves.

Sex is hardly the main point here, as if the "apple" signified the first act of intercourse as many early Christians and others have thought. But the connection is understandable, for sexual "knowing" can also alternate swiftly between loving desire and aggressive possessiveness. In any case, the text does not say that they did this out of shame. It may be inferred, of course, from the last verse in chapter 2 and shame will often be appropriate. But now, in the first place, it makes more sense to notice that their inspection of their now alienated bodies focused on those funny-looking parts that also figure in the paradox of knowledge. They are the organs that expel that which is rejected from that which has been torn from nature. Simultaneously they are the organs that restore the ecstasy of union and create new life from all this dying. What they felt, according to the text, was a new anxiety that Adam confessed to God: "I heard the sound of thee in the garden, and I was afraid, because I was naked." The act that separated Adam from God alienated him from himself by objectifying both.

Then God told them what would be the result of their grasp for knowledge. There was a curse on the bringer of the dubious good thing. The serpent must crawl upon the ground and be hated by humans. The ground, another symbol for the two-sided blessings of a good world, was also cursed. Adam and Eve (and we) were not cursed. They were informed what would be the result of their premature grasp for the fruit of the tree of good and evil. They would be alienated from each other and from the earth. They would be expelled from Eden. But God would make clothes for them and help them to bring new life into the world (Genesis 3:1). A history would result from this that leads toward a new heaven and earth. Something better than Eden can follow from their expulsion from it. Meanwhile we continue to suffer the consequences of this "original" Fall. Each of us also continues to re-experience Eden, and the tree, and the ambiguous blessings of our loss of innocence. And a final word for those of us who toil in Christian colleges: "Let not many of you become teachers, my [brothers/sisters], for you know that we who teach shall be judged with greater strictness." (James 3:1)

But that is not a truly final word. There is a promise in Adam and Eve's fear. If it is not yet that "fear of the Lord" which leads to wisdom, it is at least that fear which leads to humility and repentance. From that place awe and wonder (which is also the Greek beginning of philosophy) can lead to another aspect of wisdom's dialectic. That is the upward movement from parts to the comprehension of wholes.

More must be said about this, but for now it is enough to note one of St. Paul's celebrations of the paradoxical possibility of wisdom.

> For God has consigned all men to disobedience, that he may have mercy upon all. . . . O the depth of the riches and wisdom and knowledge of God! How unsearchable are his judgments and how inscrutable his ways! "For who has known the mind of the Lord, or who has been his counselor? "Or who has given a gift to him that he might be repaid?" For from him and through him and to him are all things. To him be glory for ever. Amen. (1 Corinthians 11:32-36)

Then, in the verses that immediately follow, he appeals to his readers "to present your bodies as a living sacrifice, holy and acceptable to God, which is your spiritual worship." Bodies are no longer the problem. So complete is the reversal that the body is no longer an "it." It is a *living* sacrifice—Paul's figure for the entire self. As belonging to the coming age, the old split is healed. Therefore, "Do not be conformed to this world but be transformed by the renewal of your mind, that you may prove what is the will of God, what is good and acceptable and perfect." (12:1-2)

THE "FALL," CHRISTIAN COLLEGES, AND FRESNO PACIFIC COLLEGE

One cannot write of God's working to transcend the Fall without writing the story of Israel and, for that matter, of all other peoples. Christians must especially write of Jesus and the Church. Nor can one write about Fresno Pacific College without addressing the Mennonite Brethren Church and its efforts to build the Kingdom of God in its own small parts of the world.

The Mennonite Brethren as the context for Fresno Pacific College

I am sometimes confounded by the ability of children to project the attributes of "neighborhood" onto what appear to me to be the cold streets and the anomic individuals of our cities. So I may not be, as I imagine, among the last of those who have grown up in Eden. I shall, nonetheless, presume to explain what that was like.

Like Adam and Eve, I can remember what it was like to live in a small, concrete community bounded in a qualitatively pre-modern "time" and in a quantitatively limited "space." The word *concrete* defines its essentially Edenic character. The second part of that word refers to something living; the prefix *con* means "together with." Together they specify a community in which the material and the social and the spiritual aspects of life are all grown together into a living organism that is *halig*. This Old English word names the quality of a good so holistic that it has not yet split apart—as the word itself did—into its material ("healthy") and spiritual ("holy") aspects.

My elders knew well enough that most of the dis-eases deriving from the Fall were well represented in the Eden I remember, but they would not have been surprised that I can claim the pre-Fall story. They had taken for granted that it was their Christian vocation to build small replicas of the Kingdom of Heaven on earth. Like the ancient Hebrews and the early Christians, my forebears instinctively understood the significance of the fact that when God decided to grow a *halig* people, he began by shaping a new kind of family with Abraham, a new kind of tribes with the twelve patriarchs, and a new kind of *ethnos* around the covenants that came through Moses and Jesus. Nor did they imagine a "docetic" Jesus forming an "invisible" church. For them the body of Christ was composed of communities made up of local clans that were, in turn, integral parts of tribes that spread out into other near and distant communities to form a people of God.

They could also understand that each of these units was more than the sum of its parts and that each had a character that was profoundly a part of each person's identity. From the point of view of these group *Geists* ("Spirits," even "Angels"), individuals were not primary. They were the "living stones" that comprised the larger "living temples," which united to form the concrete Body of Christ. The parts existed to serve the whole.

But when recognizing that the group existed for God's sake and not its own, our communities also knew that their collective aspiration to become a "holy ethnos" implied that all members had to have their own spirits claimed by God. To be a "good" member of the group was not enough. Then it became the will of the whole that each of them should respond to the Spirit's call to seek God beyond the group. Then it was true that the whole existed to serve the parts. The larger group process and the more personal individuating processes produced a particular kind of person, a particular kind of piety, and a particular kind of wisdom.

Each of us first entered the intimate space of a family before progressively "graduating" into the spaces of the clan, village, tribe, and people. In so doing we expanded to encompass the larger sets of natural and social and spiritual relations that were the vehicles of the spirits and Spirit of each. Each new level came with the bright promise of a larger becoming and each, when mastered, pointed upward and outward to a larger space. In all this one was not a *given* self experiencing all these things. Rather, one was a nexus of expanding relationships and was becoming ever more able to encompass richer dimensions of life and spirit.

Perhaps few of them achieved the piety to which they aspired, but I think that they at least sought the beauty God intended for the world and the cosmos. It was a comprehending piety, the embrace of larger realities on the way to becoming joint-heirs of Jesus Christ who sat at the right hand of God. The repose they sought in God was the confidence that the tensions and contradictions of life were resolved in the intentions of God and could be partially understood through comprehending more encompassing realities. The wisdom they sought was simply to know the mind of Christ in and through their relationships with the earth, with each other, and with the God who had given them their own gardens to tend.

When they gathered on Sunday they brought with them all that was sheltered under the sacred canopy that hovered above and around them. They offered to God the concreteness of their lives. Here they gathered together all the rhythms of nature and life with its joys and griefs as confession and petition and praise. Thus, worship was elevation and contemplation of the way things worked together for *halig*. Through this we were allowed a glimpse of ourselves and our bit of would-be paradise from God's point of view. Then we saw that we were really very small and sinful. Sometimes we trembled under the burden of what we knew should be God's righteous wrath. But we also knew that we were wonderfully made and near to the heart of God.

Growing up under such a sacred canopy included the comprehension of the levels of reality that it contained as they revealed themselves to us. The goal was to become a mature leader with the "common sense" of its greater ecology and good judgment how to enhance its *halig*. This wisdom was less the result of eating of the tree of the knowledge of good and evil than of running around in the garden, learning to tend it, and "naming" its creatures. Our comprehension of what was real and of how things worked was expressed in pithy sayings, in old saws and proverbs. As in the ancient world, wisdom was less a function of memorizing these "truths" than it was of gaining the "spiritual" gift of divining which ones applied to a given situation and how they did so.

The Scriptures were their guides to the knowledge and wisdom most worth having. But for them the text was not primarily a source of "facts" or even "truths." There was little thought of approaching it in the analytic spirit of the scientist. It was rather a story of the ways of God with human beings like themselves. The Hebrews also had been organized into families and clans and tribes. They too had mostly been farmers. They too had been exiles struggling to create a godly homeland.

The Bible was a window into a world that, like theirs, was more than the sum of its parts. Those who read it over and over lived themselves into that world. When they prayed, they could become David pleading for healing and forgiveness. When they worked, they became Adam struggling with ground that was more willing to bear weeds than wheat. When they had to make decisions about life and relationships, they moved naturally between Solomon's proverbs and their Low German ones. The world of the Bible was both real and ideal. The struggles and failures of the biblical saints might even be more sordid than their own. Yet the whole of that world was suffused with the brooding, sometimes dramatically active, presence of God. In one sense, it was not about the far past at all. It paralleled their own world, hovering above their world and intersecting with it. Its patterns could impress themselves upon their own world. They too could be God's chosen people, and so their imaginations could roam freely back and forth between that world and their own. In time, the patterns of their thinking could be molded by the biblical patterns. In the end, the most important thing they learned was not the ability to think biblical "truths." It was that they had learned to think about everything in ways corresponding to the biblical patterns. The best of them learned to think "in" the truth rather than simply "about" truths.

In part, I am trying to express what is implied in the words "common sense." Those with that gift are able to understand the whole of a thing or a process, apprehending it as if in a single picture. Some call this a "right-brained" way of perceiving; others speak of grasping a *Gestalt*. Recognizing the shape and intention of a given process, they can improve what they are given without needing a recipe.

The "thing" and the "process" that our saints were mainly about was the building of a life and a community. Through growing up in such a community and through growing their way into the vision of a people of God as presented in the Scriptures, they could comprehend its contours and shape its future. They could follow whatever guidelines were given them by the tradition and improvise where the guidelines were no longer applicable or when they conflicted in "hard cases." For difficult decisions they sat together before the

Scriptures and prayed their way into the recognition of which story or insight could best help them to solve their problem. None of this needed to have been systematically worked out. In so far as they theologized about this process, they said confidently with the early Christians, "It seemed good to the Holy Spirit and to us."

Of course, such communities do not need colleges until they reach the limits of the kind of knowledge and wisdom they "naturally" make possible. The systematic, analytic kind of thinking symbolized by the tree in Eden becomes necessary when success and growth create problems that traditional wisdom cannot answer. Inevitably, this creates a kind of systematized rationality, whether it is the bureaucratic hierarchies of Bronze Age kingdoms or the scientific, technological systems of Western modernity. Then colleges, or something like them, necessarily emerge.

The new kind of knowledge matches the nature of a new kind of society at the same time that it answers that society's needs. Its dissections match the abstractions that have emerged. In the new complexity, individuals abstract themselves (literally, they are "pulled out or away") from their concrete communities to join other abstracted persons. Together they form new kinds of societies dedicated to produce a specific product or service that has itself been abstracted from the all-grown-together round of concrete life. For the first time, *progress* becomes the goal of work and action. Instead of the common-weal, people can now aim at better products produced more efficiently for the sake of more money. Concomitantly, a third level of abstraction emerges: the discovery and rational ordering of the principles that underlie the new knowledge and technology. This rationalization speeds up the process of the discovery of more truths and the training of those who serve the new institutions of all this "progress."

Pacific Bible Institute

By the mid-1940s this new world had stealthily infiltrated the Mennonite Brethren Edens of the West Coast. The parents knew by then that their young people would have to become more educated. Many of them, however, distrusted the "Christian" colleges available to them as much or more than they did the secular ones. The Christian colleges promised to combine faith and knowledge, but the new mixture often seemed more at home in the new world than in the old Edens. Perhaps it would be wiser to expose their young people to secular institutions to satisfy their needs for secular training, and to fashion a sacred educational setting for the training they would need to become leaders in the sacred aspects of what was left of the old Edens. So they created Pacific Bible Institute in Fresno. What they failed to see was that this decision was already a product of the loss of innocence. The serpent was almost as much the institutional and intellectual father of PBI as of the University of California and Tabor College (the Christian college built by their Midwestern cousins and favored by some of their neighbors).

At PBI the *Bible* was the center of the curriculum. Such liberal arts courses as existed were justified for their servant role. Would-be ministers needed to practice the skills of speaking and writing. Sunday school teachers needed courses in psychology and education. Music was essential in worship. Basically, however, the school taught the sacred content derived from sacred Scripture that would be needed by those who would be engaged in full or part-time sacred work. What they did not understand was that not even a Bible institute could read the Bible as it had been read in the old Edens. The Scriptures had simply become the trunk and the largest limbs on the PBI tree of the knowledge of good and evil. Like other educated fundamentalists, they had transformed the Bible into a repository of abstracted facts and moral truths and doctrinal principles that revealed the structures of the now abstracted sacred sphere.

Unfortunately, students discovered that a purely sacred course of study was not even adequate for sacred careers. Churches were beginning to want pastors who would understand the kind of abstractions learned by those who were returning from colleges and universities. As a result, the more astute would-be ministers were not enrolling. Influential leaders were growing uneasy about the sacred/secular assumptions embodied in the curriculum. Those who most seriously studied the Bible discovered that breakthroughs in understanding it came from those who were also steeped in the "secular" disciplines of archeology, history, literary analysis, and linguistics. With enrollment skidding, it became clear that PBI could not survive. It rightly became Pacific College.

Pacific College

Arthur Wiebe became President in 1960, and West Coast Mennonite Brethren began coming to terms with the fact that they owned a Christian college, with all the advantages and disadvantages pertaining thereto. They also discovered that here was a Christian college with a difference. President Wiebe did not staff it with an older generation of fundamentalist teachers who had come to terms with modernist abstractiveness by turning even the Scriptures into a source of abstractions (true ones of course). Instead, he hired a group of brash young teachers bright enough to have succeeded at some of America's best universities and sophisticated enough to question many assumptions of abstractive modernity. At the same time, these young teachers were so profoundly linked into the old Edens that they wished to help to restore their concrete beauties in a form that could flourish in the modern world. In other words, they were the "grandchildren" who were no longer as hostile toward the old "naive" concreteness as were those "children" who were using fundamentalism to drag Mennonite Brethren into modernity.

They did not know how this could be done, but they were bold enough to launch a great experiment. That they slid into many mistakes enshrined in the model of the standard Christian college is not at all surprising. They did not have any good models to imitate. It is also true, I think, that they were willing to trust the wisdom and instincts that they had retained from our "pre-Fall" Edens. So they ended by shaping a college that was probably a good deal better than our more modernizing churches deserved. (I speak as one who came after the first great burst of creativeness had already shaped the content and spirit of much that we continue to enjoy.) To comment helpfully about Fresno Pacific College, I must first sketch some elements of the Christian college-model.

The Christian College Heresy

A particular kind of idolatry was the besetting sin of the communal Edens I have sketched. Their understanding could be guided by a sense of God's holy presence, but too often they followed through by asserting their own special goodness and denying God's presence in other sorts of communities. In so doing they tended to transform God into a custodian of their own ethos.

Instead of idolatry, heresy is the besetting sin of societies that have eaten deeply of the tree of the knowledge of good and evil. Heresy is especially the sin of the modern West. Christian colleges fully express the modern heresies even in the way they seek to counter the heretical spirit of the age.

The word "heresy" comes from a Greek word for a group that has abstracted itself from concreteness. It refers to a sect, or a party, or a school, as in "the *hairesis* of the Pharisees," or "the Republican *party*," or the "mercantilist *school* of economists." The characteristic truths of each of these secondary societies are not heresies because they are false. All really important heresies begin with genuine truths. The point is, simply, that they are partial. They abstract people, functions, truths, and points of view from what had once been a concrete whole. Individuals leave their primary communities sheltered under sacred canopies to join institutions structured around abstracted functions. In an almost fully abstracted society, the canopy shrinks to the family as the community's vestigial remnant. The former relational integrity of an integrated life in a concrete society is replaced by the series of more or less discrete roles the individual now plays in function-specific secondary societies.

Colleges are required by an abstracted world and mimic its structures. They are important places for thinking out and teaching the sets of specific procedures and principles that are foundational to each of the abstracted institutions and sciences. In doing this, colleges have themselves become organized into departments, each of which abstracts some aspect of knowledge for its specialized attention. Colleges, even Christian colleges, offer the fruit of the tree of good and evil and are pleased to offer tenure to the subtlest of their resident serpents.

Christian colleges even transformed biblical studies and theology into their own (departmental) abstraction. Instead of centering the curriculum around the content of the Bible, Christian colleges compensated by proclaiming Christ, as the Lord of all of life and truth, to be the center and goal of the curriculum. The "Pacific College Idea" took this step when it posited the "unity of all knowledge under God" and the correlate that there can be "no ultimate contradiction between the truth of revelation and of scholarly investigation."

That is, though *hairesis* is adopted in the institutional structure, it is denied in the Christian college's intentions. Just as the old sacred canopy enclosed all parts of the old Edens and as larger canopies arched over lesser ones until the entire world was comprehended as an ordered creation, so the foundational principles of the separate sciences were understood to be rationally comprehensible in a hierarchically structured Christian world-view.

This expectation clearly followed the Enlightenment program. The truths of each of the sciences could be derived from more basic foundational truths and their certainty could be either inherently recognized or empirically established. While the sense of the Edenic canopy was fading along with the demise of concrete communities,

Christian colleges claimed the reality of a sacred ideological canopy covering all truths. After all, in that other modernizing truism beloved by the justifiers of Christian colleges, "All truths are God's truths." Of course, it was always easier for faculty to confess their faith in God and in the *possibility* of a Christian world view than it was for them to show how their subject matter fit into the cohesive pattern that is God's point of view.

No doubt the truisms I have cited from the FPC Idea and in the preceding lines became such because they are true. But we should be wary of how we have used them. For one thing, they are strikingly harmonious with the secular Enlightenment faith in a consistent rationalist or empirical world-view. For another thing, we late-moderns have been forced again to appreciate the wisdom of the Preacher, for whom the attempt to attain complete wisdom has led to the recognition that humans cannot find it. As the philosophers from Calvin College have been teaching us, foundationalism of the sort attempted is a pious but empty promise. That is a very important and even hopeful finding. Humans may find much knowledge and even attain a limited kind of wisdom. But the typical model of the "Christian college" has been so deeply shaped by the Enlightenment version of the tree of good and evil that only a very profound rebaptism can reestablish its Christian relevance in a post-modern world.

By now, Evangelical theologians can only agree that the Bible as source of foundational truths *ought* to yield a coherent interpretation and theology within the foundationalist rationalism they had accepted. Meanwhile, life has become so complex that, as James Davison Hunter has explained, many people cannot understand the basic patterns of our own culture. They get through the day and the week, applying sets of recipes that they have learned to apply to specific circumstances and that make it possible for them to more or less "get by."[1]

CHRISTIAN COLLEGES AND THE WANING HOPE OF *HALIG*

Edens are a prerequisite for a Christian (or any) college

Both the Greeks and the Hebrews agreed that something like wonder, or awe before God, was the beginning of wisdom. They also agreed that this evoked the clear-headed sense of our inability ever to know as God knows. But it was also the key to the search for enlarged comprehensions. An initial reflex of the intimation of the beautiful and of *halig* is the rush of desire to make it one's own. For the Greeks this *eros* was the god who united heaven to earth across the chaos to engender life. To the Hebrews the Spirit of God was the power creating a living order out of the chaos. According to the Apostle Paul, this Spirit removes the veil that prevents us beholding the glory of the Lord and grants the power to metamorphose to ever higher levels of its image in us (II Corinthians 3:14-18). The second reflex of this urge to complete being is to seek the good of others. *Agape* flows from God through us as the power that fashions the City of God. True mastery is that rule which "seeketh not its own." Without the fundamental excellence of concrete love, mastery produces only a false order held briefly in place by force.

A second prerequisite is a sense of the concreteness of the realities studied and the increasingly comprehensive ability to relate abstract analyses of these realities back to the original concretions. Without the upward reach of comprehensions, the dialectical movement of wisdom is broken and we are left with the death implicit in analysis.

College teaching once made sense. When I began at Tabor in the early 1960s, students came to college from coherent neighborhoods or small towns or old-fashioned ghettos, and they had comprehended the concrete interrelatedness of several communal levels. They were ready for the abstractions that are our disciplines. They had a more than nodding acquaintance with a natural ecosystem that science classes helped to explain. They had confronted the verities of life and love and death that the humanities celebrate. When a historian or sociologist or political thinker expounded the theories that throw light on human institutions, they could apply those insights to the communities they had known. Curricula did not have to be coherent; insights could come in any order. The student's home-grown world-view furnished the spaces into which our jumble of puzzle-pieces could be fitted.

Unfortunately, colleges today — even Christian colleges — cannot assume that students arrive with either the fear of God (in the required sense) or with the ability to apprehend concrete totalities. In the past, we could take for granted that students came from small, primary communities and had direct experience of basic facets of the life of their communities and a "common sense" of their coherence. They came to college expecting to add new knowledge and insights to their common sense and to achieve an imaginative grasp of larger concretions. Though recognition of finitude might warn them of the impossibility of fully comprehending larger totalities, the ability to imagine what such a grasp would be like and the drive to move toward it was, I believe, made possible by earlier experiences of more limited wholes. So long as there is at least an intuitive sense of that larger reality, abstractions can point to the truth they only partially engage.

Furthermore, colleges in the past offered a curriculum that at least seemed comprehensible. Even the entering student could envision its confines, apprehend it as a body of learning, and aspire to at least a conventional mastery of the whole. The remnants of the classical curriculum (from longer ago), with its quadrivium and trivium and its reading of selected biblical and Greek and Latin classics, provided a "General Education" that all shared and that furnished the basis for a civilizing discourse. It also allowed for the development of good judgment on the concerns of the commonwealth.

It is important to understand that a limited content can be a rich one. Narrowness comes in different packages. Small primary communities must contain the basic elements of life, must be a microcosm. On the other hand, the scattered functions of a complex city can prevent one from ever discovering some basic aspects of reality, and a comprehensive common sense may never emerge. The liberating power of a limited curriculum that features close readings of the classics of Western civilization should not be underestimated. Intelligent limitation is essential to the apprehension of the heights and depths of that which inevitably will exceed our total comprehension. Breadth of knowledge, except for the very gifted, easily correlates with a shallow mind.

It is also the case that a multi-dimensional experience and education (even if of limited breadth) was conducive to the development of good judgment. An unbounded curriculum, itself a contradiction in terms, leads to the amassing of facts and insights — but wisdom is lost. Wisdom and judgment depend upon knowing how bits of knowledge fit into the larger whole and how insights are applied so that the balanced tensions permitting health and creativity can be maintained. There is a wisdom that emerges from a sense of tradition. There is even a gift of discernment given to saints who have practiced the (apparently) narrowest sphere of all — the relation of the self to itself and to its God in prayer. Perhaps the greatest depth of comprehension is possible only within the "narrowest" of limits.

West of Eden

It may literally be impossible to make sense of knowledge (except as tools for the attainment of mundane and immediate ends) when the sense of the appropriate concretions is lost. Every course and department of even the largest university is based upon abstractions from reality. One way to abstract is to isolate particular elements of the larger whole ("In this course we deal with the physics of light."). Another way is to study aspects of the whole ("In this department we deal with the material basis of reality."). Another way is to study the whole from a particular point of view ("In this university we study everything in terms of the metaphysics of dialectical materialism."). Yet another way is to analyze the appropriate methodology for the study of a given content ("In this course we analyze historiographical techniques."). One can argue that the modern university fails to teach mastery both because it knows too much and because what it knows is parceled into the specialist domains of departments and divisions, and then is taught from an often unrecognized ideological bias.

In this context, "education" increasingly becomes a second-order abstraction from sets of abstractions. So long as the original reality has previously been apprehended, the abstractions can add to its comprehension. But when the sense of the larger reality fades, the sequences of analyses themselves become the quasi-concreteness from which further analysis springs. Then contemplations are "of" the process of contemplations — like movies about the making of movies. We need not argue that this is illegitimate. But I do argue that research universities organized for this purpose, or even small liberal arts colleges cloned in their image, are not appropriate places for undergraduates who intend mastery. Moreover, the extended process can quickly become demonic. To paraphrase Reinhold Niebuhr, since we can infinitely abstract from reality, we are tempted to forget that we are neither infinite nor abstract.

Finally, we must note that fewer students (or faculty) have experienced coherent primary communities. The world increasingly presents itself in abstracted, functional, and incoherent fragments. We are reduced to trying to center our lives in one or more such fragments. As specialists we teach our fragments to students who hope that at least one set of them will make them well-paid functionaries in a bewildering world from which they will nightly flee to the very small private life of the "nuclear" family, which the Greeks thought "idiotic," which the Hebrews considered the foundation for a larger communal identity, and which Jesus feared as a potentially idolatrous barrier to the search for the Kingdom of God.

For many years American education has mirrored, even led, this fragmentation. Its curricula have been "enriched" by an incredible explosion of information and theories. More and more it has been left to the students to try to forge coherence out of the bewildering array of choices available to them. Meanwhile their teachers, freshly minted from graduate schools where they learned the complications of a single mode of abstraction or the complexities of several modes applied to one aspect of reality, have no inkling of educational statesmanship. Lacking a vision of what sort of coherence beginning collegians should be offered, they do the best they can by teaching ever more esoteric courses — reproducing for undergraduates what they learned in graduate research universities. In turn, the collegians go out to impose watered-down versions of that for high schoolers, while grade-school teachers try to compensate for the failure of the schools of education to show them the glorious opportunity to become master teachers by enrolling in programs that offer to make them specialists. Academic enrichment often turns out to mean the mere trick of learning more content at earlier ages. Libraries aspire to create collections so large that students are too intimidated to enter, since the chances of finding the "right" book are vanishingly small.

Worse yet, the Christian colleges themselves increasingly undermine the churches that send them their best youth so that they can become the leaders their communities need to flourish in a world becoming more complex, more promising, and more threatening. When it became clear that many of these youth would not return to their own communities, these colleges made this another reason for their existence. Here the youth would learn the abstracted skills needed for success in the larger world. Surely they would preach to that larger world the abstracted truths the home and college affirmed.

Thus abstraction, and *hairesis*, triumphs. Too few students return to their home churches and almost no one returns with the vision of making the church itself an ongoing "graduate school" for reflection and action in seeking first "the Kingdom of God and its righteousness." Nor is the kind of Bible study learned in abstracted Bible departments able to survive the journey back home. The best students may learn to dissect the text and to discover many wonderful truths in it. But the Scriptures have mostly ceased to be the entry to a dynamic tradition of communal wrestling with each other and with God. Having failed to show how the critical study of Scripture could free and enrich the community's own struggle toward *halig*, the initial shock induced by some findings of critical scholarship cannot be overcome, and biblical scholarship itself is seen as heresy.

Arthur F. Holmes, whom I take to be an able and typical spokesperson for such colleges, has many wise things to say in *The Idea of a Christian College*.[2] But I think it revelatory that despite his recognition that learning requires community and relationships, he betrays no apparent recognition that concreteness is an essential basis for both. So it is also relevant that nearly all of his approximately thirty references to "church" are mere "asides." Nowhere is there discussion of the direct service to its own welfare that a church has the right to expect from a Christian college and from its graduates. It may also be relevant that he writes from Wheaton, Illinois, quite probably the "para-church" capital of the world. So endemic is modern abstractionism that many of the leading Christian colleges are themselves "para-church." Even denominational colleges softpedal their affiliation while pointing their students toward parachurch Christian service. All this is to be expected, of course, in a world in which churches, having ceased to be centers for a concrete ethos, have become congregations — abstracted secondary institutions servicing the abstracted "spiritual" aspect of people's lives.

Fresno Pacific College as a "Mennonite" Christian college

Adam and Eve were not allowed to return to Eden. They should not even have wanted to. The Kingdom of God lies beyond Eden, on the other side of the Fall. Its possibility requires a continuing, though chastened, eating from the tree of the knowledge of good and evil. Toward that goal, Abraham and Jacob-Israel and Moses were charged with the promise and the task of creating the kind of families, tribes, and people that could prepare for and model a nation of priests. The first Christians asserted that Jesus extended this promise and claim to all peoples. Even the heirs of the Anabaptists set busily to work to create concrete Edens, and then confronted their youth with the goal of comprehending and transcending them so that they could directly confront the God who judged all idolatries and heresies. Having been forgiven and healed, they could then choose freely to seek the *halig* of their own concrete communities or they could go outward in mission to create others.

Perhaps Fresno Pacific College has imbibed so deeply of the models of the liberal arts and Christian college that it cannot recover from contemporary *haireses*. There is enough in the FPC Idea to warrant the claim that we have unthinkingly accepted the old clichés. Certainly the self-study prepared for the most recent accreditation visit (1994) can be used to argue that. (But that would be unfair. The standards and forms insisted on by accrediting agencies force the appearance of heresy on *every* school.) There is little evidence that our churches are resisting the modern move to become mere congregations.

But there is another possibility. Our ethnic and rural heritage has given many of us a sense of the shape of concrete communities and an appreciation of the beauty of what is whole and holy. Our religious history grants to us the capacity to look critically at the spirit of our age. We have a genuine, if confused, conviction that the liberal arts are basic to an authentic education and that a limited curriculum may compensate in depth for what it lacks in breadth. We have attracted teachers from other traditions whose life experiences and/or intellectual development have taught them communal values and a contextual approach to education. Perhaps more importantly, students, staff, and faculty forge a communal style that is more concrete than some students have ever experienced. One side of our entrepreneurial style is the courage to discover (and rediscover?) what is educationally significant.

It may be, therefore, that we can reaffirm an older and truly Christian search for knowledge in a form that is viable for a distracted world. Perhaps we can affirm the profundity of the Hebrew tradition of wisdom (with its proverbs and figures and riddles) and begin with an upward-striving fear of the Lord that balances the downward-pulling analytics of the tree of the knowledge of good and evil. With a salutary humility, we then will be able to celebrate with Paul:

> Oh, the depth of the riches both of the wisdom and knowledge of God! How unsearchable are his judgments, and his ways past finding out! For who hath known the mind of the Lord? Or who hath been his counselor? Or who hath first given to him, and it shall be recompensed unto him again? For of him, and through him, and to him, are all things: to whom be glory forever. Amen. (Romans 11:33-36)

With this knowledge, we will be more aware of ourselves in place and in time. We are planted in an undistinguished section of a moderate-sized city as a small college belonging to a small part of a tiny Mennonite denomination with a short history and limited resources. Yet, whether from faith or need, we testify that it is with God that we have to do — as was true of others who have existed in other places and times.

Paul also knew the need for modesty (though he did not reckon with the need to be more modestly and deliberately gender inclusive). Two verses later, he writes:

> For I say, through the grace given unto me, to every man that is among you, not to think of himself more highly than he ought to think, but to think soberly, according as God hath dealt to every man the measure of faith. For as we have many members in one body, and all members have not the same office, So we, being many, are one body in Christ, and every one members one of another. (Romans 12:3-5)

Without presuming to possess a text that automatically answers all our questions or a comprehensively true theology/philosophy that allows us to know as God knows, we may, nonetheless, explore reverently the dialogue called forth by God's creating, sustaining, and redeeming acts. Into this continuing dialogue with God and with all others we too are privileged to enter. For, as Paul then insists, this concrete unity that is the body of Christ is graced with the different gifts given to its members, which bring knowledge and all the other needed fruits to create a holy and healthy society.

That brings us to the most troubling paradox of all. A Christian college is a special creation of the church. It is designed to play a specific role in the larger mission of the church. But modern churches are becoming congregations. They too are succumbing to the abstracting, functionalizing spirit of the age. So those of us who are inspired by the call to serve the various levels of a concrete people of God are increasingly driven to create here the *halig* that no longer characterizes the congregations from which we come. But how can the abstraction that an abstracted church creates to do an abstracted job with young members who are abstracted from their abstracting communities for a brief four years abstracted from their lives become a concrete community? Until congregations again become churches that seek to become concrete parts of the Kingdom of God, we can hardly help them or their youth even if we "succeed" at our own mission. To the extent that we try to do so, we may even turn out to be at odds with the congregations we are supposed to serve.

Though this was not always articulated well, those who built Fresno Pacific College and many of us who now serve here, were the product of Christian communities and grew up with this "in our bones." An increasingly fragmented culture is driving many to a new appreciation of the need for concrete communal structures. The least we can do is to analyze the "signs of the times," using the best insights offered by the tree of knowledge, and to bear witness to the gospel out of that fear of God which keeps us hopeful and honest — and which gives us the courage to renew not only our minds but also the structures by which they have been too much shaped.

> I beseech you therefore, brethren, by the mercies of God, that ye present your bodies a living sacrifice, holy, acceptable unto God, which is your reasonable service. And be not conformed to this world, but be ye transformed by the renewing of your mind, that ye may prove what is that good and acceptable, and perfect, will of God. (Romans 12:1-2)

NOTES

1. James Davison Hunter, *American Evangelicalism: Conservative Religion and the Quandary of Modernity* (New Brunswick, NJ.: Rutgers Univ. Press, 1983, 10. This book and Hunter's sequel, *Evangelicalism: The Coming Generation* (Chicago: The University of Chicago Press, 1987) are extremely important analyses of Evangelicalism's "bargaining with modernity." In this latter book Hunter argues that students in the best of the Christian colleges are rapidly succumbing to the spirits of the age. The almost morbid fear of conservative Christians that their colleges "will go the way of Harvard, Yale, and Princeton" is justified. Having already adopted structural and epistemological *haireses* it is quite inevitable that other heresies will follow.

2. Arthur F. Holmes, *The Idea of a Christian College*, revised ed. (Grand Rapids, Mich.: William B. Eerdmans, 1989).

Chapter 4

"Community" and the Pacific College Idea: Dilemmas in the Institutionalization of Religion

Robert Enns

The survival of recognizably Protestant colleges therefore seems to depend on the survival within the larger society of Protestant enclaves whose members believe passionately in a way of life radically different from that of the majority, and who are both willing and able to pay for a brand of higher education that embodies their vision. Such enclaves still exist, but they are few in number.

-Christopher Jencks and David Riesman, 1968[1]

Fresno Pacific College in its fiftieth year is not the institution that it was in the earlier decades of its history. One theme, however, that has continued through the decades of change is the vision of the institution as an expression of Christian "community."

There are two alternative perspectives that might be useful in telling and evaluating the story of "community" at Fresno Pacific College. "Secularization" provides a commonly utilized interpretive framework for reflecting on change in American higher education. The notion of "dilemma" offers another way of interpreting the process of change in religious institutions, including the Christian college. Religious institutions must deal with structural dilemmas for which there can be no ultimate resolution. Changes in the nature of the Fresno Pacific College "community" may better be interpreted as dynamic, on-going relationships between sets of conflicting religious visions and institutional realities, both poles of which are positive and essential to the nature of the institution, than as "secularization," a (decline) from sacred (positive) to secular (negative) qualities.

THE "SECULARIZATION" THESIS

The "secularization" interpretive model has a long and venerable history in sociological thought, from Max Weber's notions of "rationality" and "disenchantment" of nature through Robert Bellah's analysis of the "privatization" of religion in America. The concept has been applied in studies of evangelicals and Mennonites and to the larger socio-religious environment.

Even prior to the work of Christopher Jencks and David Riesman, the secularization model was widely used to characterize change in American higher education. In 1952 historian Richard Hofstadter wrote, "There are several major themes that command the attention of the historian of American higher education, but among these the oldest and the longest sustained is the drift toward secularism."[2] American church historian George Marsden points to the very close relationship that existed between American cultural protestantism and public higher education even into the twentieth century. A widely held consensus concerning linkages between the church and the public universities included several expectations. The college or university president was expected to be an active churchman; students were expected to attend chapel services; a "capstone" course in ethics was generally a required part of the curriculum; and the college, acting "*en loco parentis*," was expected to discipline students for violations of commonly held standards of decency. Evidence of this religious legacy remains materially visible even today in the official logos and on the formal dedicatory plaques found on many university campuses (both public and historically church-affiliated) across the country.[3]

A general definition of "secularization" is the removal of institutions from ecclesiastical control and the exclusion or relegation of religious symbols and practices to the margins of institutional life. Marsden suggests several reasons for the recent secularization of public higher education in America: a growing commitment to technological development that led to professionalization and specialization both outside and within the universities; a scientific version of the enlightenment perspective that was adopted by most American intellectuals, including many liberal protestant church and educational leaders; and a growing acceptance of both the reality and the positive value of cultural pluralism in America.[4]

In 1963, Catholic commentator Charles F. Donovan, S.J., commented on this process within his own tradition:

> The history of American higher education is a sad story of loss of faith by religious institutions. The presence in so many parts of the country of secularized, non-religious, at times even antireligious institutions whose foundations were inspired by religious zeal and apostolic motives seems almost like empirical proof of the contention of positivists that faith and intelligence are incompatible.[5]

Many commentators note that evangelical Bible and Christian liberal arts colleges exhibit a variation on this theme of developmental secularization. Some trace a series of stages in a transition through which the evangelical colleges move from the margins toward the center of the American cultural and academic mainstream. Thomas Askew, a Gordon College historian, identifies three phases of development in the history of the evangelical colleges: "The Insular, Church-focused Institution"; "Corporate Definition, Consolidation, and Credentialing"; and "Professionalization, Networks, and Theoretical Understanding."[6]

Historians have viewed Mennonite higher education in this same light. James Juhnke, to cite but one such scholar, traces three generations of leadership in Mennonite higher education: a "founding generation," which was "preoccupied with relationships to a conservative, rural, often German-speaking, constituency"; a "middle generation," which "managed a drive to institutional accreditation which met the need of the progressive wings of the Mennonite subculture for legitimation and respectability"; and a more recent "postwar generation" of leaders, who "entered upon an era of professionalization and bureaucratization which matched trends toward affluence, urbanization, and specialization in the rapidly acculturating Mennonite communities." Juhnke concludes:

> A number of scholars have recently chronicled and analyzed the secularization of American higher education in the 19th and 20th centuries. Mennonites were late arrivers on the scene of American

Protestant denominational development. It is worth asking whether Mennonite colleges are belatedly recapitulating a mainline Protestant process and succumbing to the same secularizing forces which separated so many American Protestant colleges from their sponsoring churches.[7]

DILEMMAS IN THE INSTITUTIONALIZATION OF RELIGION

Most commentators who utilize the secularization perspective do not assume that secularization necessarily requires a unilinear progression in a fixed direction through inevitable stages of development. Institutions follow varied routes along the way toward different forms of adaptation, growth, or demise. The notion of "dilemma," often used with the secularization model, permits a more nuanced perspective on processes of institutional change. Marsden, for example, does recognize a genuine dilemma that American protestants inevitably confront in their endeavors in higher education. Principles such as equity, tolerance, and voluntarism conflict with any claims to dominance or privilege on the part of a protestant religious establishment. The issue was focused by the question of the place of Jewish students and faculty within the public (but protestant-oriented) university: justice and equity seemed to require the free participation of Jewish faculty and students in public university life without prejudice or discrimination. But to do so meant the end of the dominant cultural-religious consensus that protestantism historically had provided. The ideal of cultural relativism that seemed to provide a way to resolve this dilemma contributed, actually, to the secularization of American colleges and universities as well as the larger church and society.[8]

More recently, the journal *Crosscurrents* presented studies of four colleges under the title "Living in Ambiguity: Religiously Identified Colleges Today."[9] At Brandeis, the tensions involve (ethnic) Jewishness and (religious) Judaism in a college that is committed both to religious ecumenicity and cultural diversity. Wheaton College has historically faced tensions between its commitments to excellence in "liberal arts" education and a historical tradition of theological and cultural fundamentalism. Guilford College struggles to realize continuity with the Quaker tradition of decision-making through "a sense of the meeting" in an institution populated by administration, faculty and students who have been socialized into a more individualistic, enlightenment model of relationships. Catholic colleges struggle with tensions between having "an open mind and heart toward all cultures" and the "closed culture" of episcopal authority. "It is safe, in other words, to say that most, perhaps all religiously affiliated colleges live in a state of vexing ambiguity."[10]

Many studies of Mennonite religious institutions have also utilized the notion of "dilemma." Mennonite sociologist Leland Harder, for example, saw a dilemma in Mennonite commitment to both separation from the world and ministry to the world. These contradictory impulses, both essential components of Mennonite religious identity, were an on-going source of structural "disequilibrium" in Mennonite institutional life.[11] Peter Hamm, Mennonite Brethren sociologist and missiologist, saw in the history of the Mennonite Brethren an on-going conflict between "sacralization" (by which he meant authentic spiritual breakthroughs) and "secularization" (the loss of religious authenticity that came with the institutional forms through which those spiritual breakthroughs were expressed socially and culturally).[12]

The ideas of dilemma and ambiguity offer a more fruitful interpretive perspective on the history of "community" at Fresno Pacific College than the more commonly utilized secularization model. More specifically, the identity and mission of Fresno Pacific College expressed in the college's statements of institutional vision and theological orientation include commitments to divergent and, perhaps, contradictory notions, both of which are, paradoxically, essential to the nature of "community" at Fresno Pacific College. These ideological dilemmas are compounded by the changing composition of the campus community as the numbers of persons, diversity of programs, and demographic characteristics of the institution have grown and changed.

INSTITUTIONAL IDENTITY: IDEOLOGICAL AMBIGUITIES

From its inception Fresno Pacific College has held that "Christian" is a unifying center of its institutional identity and a foundation for the "community" that it seeks to realize. But like the founding Mennonite Brethren denomination, Christian identity includes multiple theological traditions. More specifically, it is an institution of the Mennonite Brethren religious movement, which traces its spiritual parentage to Menno Simons and other sixteenth-century Anabaptists. But the denomination also holds membership in the National Association of Evangelicals, and beginning in 1948 Pacific Bible Institute became affiliated with the fundamentalist Accrediting Association of Bible Institutes and Bible Colleges.

The continuing legacy of this fundamentalist dimension of the college's ideological identity is clearly apparent in a twelve-article statement of theological orientation, some version of which has appeared in every catalog since 1945. The statement was initially called "An Abridged Statement of Faith," because it was a condensed and edited version of the 1902 Mennonite Brethren Confession of Faith. From 1954 to 1956 the articles were called "Statement of Faith" and then for four years, "Confession of Faith." In 1962 the title was changed to "Statement of Doctrinal Policy." The title "Theological Orientation of the College" continues in use from 1968 through the 1994-1995 catalog.

The content of the "Statement of Theological Orientation" affirms many of the core ideas that have characterized American fundamentalism since the inception of the movement early in this century. It includes phrases such as "infallible Word of God," "imminent, personal and visible" return of Christ, the "Great Commission" as the "supreme mission of the church of this age," and "a state of eternal punishment for all unbelievers." It is interesting, however, that the statement has not included some terms and positions to which other institutions (including, until 1992, Wheaton College) have committed themselves, such as the "Biblical inerrancy, eschatological premillenialism and special divine creation of human beings."[13]

Further evidence of the aggressive fundamentalism that has been one element in the college's identity may be seen in the New Testament text that appeared in the early catalogs as the school's motto: "Earnestly contending for the faith (Jude 3)." In the catalogs for 1965 through 1967 (after which it is dropped altogether) the motto was softened to read ". . . for the faith."

Another declaration similar in tone appeared for several years on the title page of the catalogs of the Pacific Bible Institute and Pacific College:

A School
That seeks to make Christ preeminent
Bible authority final
The presence of the Holy Spirit Real
And makes no apology for being
Biblical
Evangelical
Missionary

The "Fresno Pacific College Idea" statement of institutional identity as formulated in the 1960s differed significantly in both content and tone from the theological statement. It first appeared in the 1969-1970 college catalog as a replacement of an earlier list of institutional goals and objectives. The Idea statement expresses a more ecumenically inclusive definition of "Christian" than the Theological Orientation Statement. It includes phrases such as "God's self-disclosure of himself in Jesus Christ and in the record of Scripture" and "the unity of all knowledge under God." The college perceives "no ultimate contradiction between the truth of revelation and of scholarly investigation" and it "considers a primary goal to be the integration of faith and learning." The revised Idea adds references to "the sovereignty of God and the triumph of his kingdom" and "the presence of His Spirit in the life of the church." It generally substitutes more ecumenically inclusive and irenic language for the more defensive and polemic terminology of the Theological Orientation Statement.

The original Idea statement indicated explicitly that "Pacific College is an Anabaptist-Mennonite College" and it provided a concise outline of the meaning of that idea. The 1982 revision repeats many of the same points. Both definitions of Anabaptism include affirmation of the Lordship of Christ over all of life, the authority of Scripture for all matters of faith and life, the voluntary nature of Christian faith, Christian life as a life of discipleship, the church as the community of redeemed people, and the importance of the practice of love.

The 1982 revision translates several of these points into different language. "Anabaptist-Mennonite" becomes "the Believers' Church tradition." "Promotion of peace and non-resistance" becomes "the practice of reconciliation and love in settings of violence, oppression, and injustice." The 1982 revision omits explicit reference to the Christian primitivism ("the college seeks to recapture the faith and life of the early Christian church") of the 1966 version. But it includes in this context a pietistic affirmation of "the development of spiritual maturity through the disciplines of prayer, study, and meditation." In both versions of the Idea, the influence of Harold S. Bender's seminal essay "The Anabaptist Vision" is unmistakable.

In spite of (or because of?) this profession of commitment to the Anabaptist-Mennonite heritage of the college, both versions of the Idea commit the college to inclusive relations with persons from other religious traditions. During its early years, "a definite confession of Christ as Savior" and a recommendation from a pastor were required for admission. But the institution suggested its openness to certain types of diversity even then by declaring itself to be "non-sectarian," meaning that students from other Christian denominations were admissible. In 1962 the boundaries became even more open to diversity: "While standing without reservation on the teachings of the inspired Word of God, the Bible, no attempt is made to force upon students views of a denominational or sectarian nature. No religious qualifications are established for entrance."

The 1966 Idea contained a separate article, "Pacific College is a Non-Sectarian College," interpreted to mean that "Religious discrimination of a narrow sectarian nature is not imposed in the admissions policy of the college. Anyone wanting a Christian education is invited to join Pacific in a quest for meaning and wholeness of life." The revised Idea expresses this same inclusiveness in affirming that "the Gospel transcends the limitations of all cultures and ideologies" and indicates that the college "invites persons from various cultural, national, ethnic, and religious settings and backgrounds to participate in the educational experience."

The manner in which the college has used the Idea statement differs significantly from the functions of the theological statement. Although the theological statement has appeared in the catalog in some version since 1945 and has been edited and moved from one location to another in the catalog and other college materials, it has not systematically been reviewed, modified, or reaffirmed by either the college or the sponsoring Pacific District Conference of Mennonite Brethren Churches. This is in spite of the fact that the larger General Conference of Mennonite Brethren Churches revised its Confession of Faith in 1975; that an alternative, officially adopted short version of the Confession of Faith is used by some other Mennonite Brethren institutions; and in spite of the substantial changes that both the Pacific District Conference and the institution have experienced during the last fifty years.

The one place where reference is made to the theological statement is at the point of entrance into the college community. Appointments of full-time faculty, administration, and members of the Board are made only after the candidate affirms (in writing) personal identification with the theological statement. Adjunct faculty members are expected to be "supportive" of the college's theological orientation statement even though they may not be able to affirm the statement personally. The theological statement is included in application materials for undergraduate (but not graduate or professional development) students, though students are not required to subscribe to it as a condition of admission. A primary function of the theological statement, then, is to provide a screening, boundary-maintenance mechanism for eliminating prospective college leadership, faculty, and staff who cannot profess identification with this component of the college's religious heritage.

The Idea, on the other hand, has played an intentional and "foundational" role in the creation and evaluation of institutional programs and practices. Following the "utopian" tradition, which sociologist Calvin W. Redekop identifies as the central feature of the Anabaptist-Mennonite movement,[14] the Idea "is a guide for the future." The Idea, rather than purely pragmatic or market considerations or precedents set by other institutions, should shape the institution. Theory and practice should be brought together in campus programs that are (in the words of the original Idea) both "experimental" and "prophetic." This ambitious idealism has, at times, been the source of innovative programs. For example, undergraduate programs such as the mentor-collegium counselling program, the College Hour program, and an academic calendar that included five-unit courses that met four days a week (leaving Wednesdays free for "community" activities) were explicitly linked to the vision of community that was central in the Idea statement. Similarly, relatively egalitarian and participatory administrative structures and practices, and a comparatively low ratio of difference between highest and lowest faculty salaries were understood to be expressive of the institution's vision of Christian community.

Since its inception, then, Fresno Pacific College (like other religious institutions) has struggled with theological ambiguities in its attempts to define the ideological center for the community that it seeks to realize. A shared commitment to being "Christian" is foundational to institutional self-understanding. References to the Christian nature of the college appear in every written statement in which the college (or any of its schools, divisions, or programs) attempts to articulate its identity or purpose. But ambiguity concerning what "Christian" means is clear in the two statements that have appeared in each catalog since 1969: the fundamentalist "Theological Orientation" statement and the more ecumenical and Anabaptist-Mennonite "Idea" statement. Even within the Idea, a combination of generic "Christian" and particular "Anabaptist-Mennonite" (or "Believers Church Tradition") emphases co-exist. Both versions of the Idea statement commit the college to *both* a common religious center *and* openness to students from diverse religious and cultural traditions.

The changes in the content of — and in relationships between — the Idea and the statement of theological orientation reflect an on-going tension between two diverse understandings of the ideological foundation for community at the college. The original Pacific College Idea statement represented a transition away from the more exclusive fundamentalism reflected in the twelve articles selectively excerpted from the 1902 Mennonite Brethren Confession of Faith. But both visions have continued to coexist within the "Christian" center that provides one foundational element for the realization of the community to which the institution has aspired from its beginnings to the present.

DILEMMAS OF UNITY AND DIVERSITY:
COMPOSITION OF THE COMMUNITY

In its early stages of development, the college realized community through a common Christian vision and a series of shared academic and co-curricular programs and practices. Community was sustained, also, through a campus population in which students, faculty, staff, administration, board, and supporting constituency shared a common ethno-religious heritage. Community was not only ideological and programmatic. It was grounded, also, in informally shared Russian Mennonite immigrant traditions, including networks of both spiritual and biological kinship. As the college expanded the circles of publics that it served, the inadequacy of its small constituent base to support the programs that it generated became more apparent. It is no surprise, then, that the composition of the college community has changed as the number of persons who choose to receive the increasingly varied services that the college provides has grown. Growth and diversity are apparent in every sphere of the institution: student bodies, faculty, administration, board, sponsoring constituency, institutional affiliations, financial donors, and in the religious, gender, and ethnic composition of the college community.

Program Diversification and Numerical Growth

Table I shows the diversification of programs and growth in the numbers of students enrolled for selected years 1966-1993:[15] Fresno Pacific College began in 1944 as a small Bible Institute with thirty-four students and six faculty. By the fall of 1966, the year after accreditation by the Western Association of Schools and Colleges as a four-year liberal arts college, undergraduate enrollment had grown to 257. During the 1970-1971 academic year, the college began to offer a fifth-year teacher credential program and in-service courses for professional educators (since re-named the Professional Development Division). A graduate program in education was initiated during the decade of the 1970s and a Degree Completion Program was approved in 1989.

Table I
Number of Students and Full-Time Faculty:
Selected Years, 1966-1993

Year	Under-grad	Teacher Ed.	Profess. Develop.	Grad.	Degree Comp.	Total	Faculty (full-time)
1966	257	0	0	0	0	257	17
1971	411	21	4,902	0	0	5,334	31
1976	436	17	5,734	34	0	6,221	37
1981	358	25	5,061	336	0	5,780	34
1986	410	131	5,794	505	0	6,840	50
1991	513	174	11,005	646	61	12,399	76
1993	642	129	11,883	674	130	13,458	91

Undergraduate, teacher education and graduate enrollment figures indicate the number of students enrolled at the beginning of the Fall Term.
Professional Development enrollment figures for 1971-1976 give the total number of registrants in courses offered. Professional Development enrollment figures for 1981 through 1993 indicate the number of unduplicated individuals who registered for at least one course during the academic year, fall, winter, summer.
Full-time faculty figures for 1981 and 1986 exclude three persons who were part of the faculty on the Modesto extension campus.

The extensive circle of persons served by the college is shown in the fact that between 1986 and 1994, 52,061 different ("unreplicated") individuals enrolled in at least one unit from the Professional Development Division.

The 1966-1967 catalog listed seventeen full-time faculty (including administrators such as president, dean, registrar, and librarian). Ten years later, the catalog for 1975-1976 listed thirty-four full time faculty. The full time faculty grew to forty-six by 1985. The 1994-1995 catalog lists ninety-four full-time faculty and administrators. The implications of this rate of program diversification and numerical growth for the nature of community life and institutional identity are inestimable. But other forms of diversification have accompanied program expansion and numerical growth.

Denominational Affiliations

During the early years of its history, Pacific Bible Institute was operated by and primarily for the Mennonite Brethren Conference. Most (but not all) students and faculty were religiously and ethnically Mennonite Brethren. The 1945 catalog indicates that the institution was "not sectarian" in its admission policy, meaning that members of other denominations were admissible. But a "definite confession of Christ as Savior" and a recommendation from a pastor were required of all students. A perusal of the early catalogs indicates that faculty, too, were predominantly (but not exclusively) Mennonite Brethren.

Some of the patterns of change in the religious preferences and affiliations of members of the college community are summarized in Table II. This table shows that in 1966, 57 percent of undergraduate students listed Mennonite Brethren as their denominational preference. This represents a decrease from 81 percent in 1960, but a numerical increase from 83 to 146 Mennonite Brethren students during those same years. The total number of Mennonite Brethren students, in fact, reached its all-time high the following year (1967) when the college enrolled 190 Mennonite Brethren students (51 percent of the student body of 371). By 1985 the total number of Mennonite Brethren students had decreased by one half to eighty-four and these students represented only 20 percent of undergraduate enrollment. During the twenty-five years from 1960 to 1985, then, the Mennonite Brethren presence in the student population decreased from approximately four out of five students to fewer than one in five.

Table II also presents two indicators of the Mennonite Brethren affiliation of faculty members. Information in the 1966 catalog concerning the seventeen full-time members of the faculty shows that 65 percent had earned an undergraduate degree or certificate in a Mennonite institution of higher learning, an indication of formal socialization into the Mennonite ethos. Table II shows that only 34 percent of the ninety-four full-time faculty listed in the catalog for

1994 included a program in a Mennonite college as part of their undergraduate education. The Table shows, also, that 88 percent of the faculty listed in the 1966 catalog appeared to be ethnic Mennonites. By 1994 a bare majority (51 percent) of the faculty had an ethnic Mennonite background. The direction of change is even more clearly apparent when faculty who are listed in the 1994 catalog who were *not* listed in the 1985-1986 catalog ("new" faculty) are compared with faculty who are listed in both the 1985 and most recent catalogs ("long-time faculty"). Of the sixty-three "new faculty" added to the catalog since 1985-1986, 30 percent list an undergraduate program in a Mennonite college and 37 percent are ethnic Mennonites. Of the thirty-one "long-time faculty," in contrast, 42 percent list an undergraduate program in a Mennonite college and 80 percent are ethnic Mennonites.

Table II
Mennonite Affiliations: Faculty and Undergraduate Students,
for Selected Years, 1966-1994

Year	% MB denomination preference (undergraduate)	% faculty completed program in Mennonite college	% faculty with Mennonite ethnic background
1966	57%	65%	88%
1970	37%	63%	97%
1975	30%	54%	87%
1980	31%	41%	91%
1985	21%	39%	70%
1993	17%	34%	51%

Denominational preference data for 1966-1985 reported by Registrar for students enrolled in Fall Term. Data for 1993 from Admissions office for new students only, Fall Term.

Faculty education data drawn from catalog vitae that list undergraduate work in a Mennonite college.

Faculty ethnic background data based on personal information about faculty listed in catalog.

Table III indicates the direction in which undergraduate student religious preferences have changed as the proportion of Mennonite Brethren students has declined:

Table III
Denominational Preferences
of new undergraduate students, fall semesters

Denominational group	1991	1993
Mennonite Brethren	23%	17%
Baptist	22%	14%
Catholic	11%	11%
Charismatic (Assembly of God, Foursquare, Nazarene, Pentecostal)	11%	11%
Mainline (Congregational Episcopalian, Lutheran, Methodist, Presbyterian)	9%	9%
Non-specific (None, non-denominational, Protestant)	17%	30%
Other denominational (Church of Christ, Church of God, Covenant, Evangelical Free, Mormon, other Mennonite)	7%	7%
Total	100% N=141	99% N=236

In 1993, the largest number of new students (30 percent) responded with generic categories including "non-denominational," "protestant," or "none." Mennonite Brethren make up the largest grouping of students (17 percent in 1993) who indicated a specific denominational affiliation. "Baptists" have consistently provided the second largest number of students who indicate a preference for a specific denomination (though "Baptist" does not distinguish the various Baptist denominations). Baptist enrollment reached a peak in 1976 when 113 Baptist students enrolled, 24 percent of total enrollment. Catholic student enrollment increased steadily from the time of the enrollment of the first Catholic student in 1963 to 1983 when Catholic student enrollment exceeded 10 percent of the student population. For several years Catholic students have formed the third largest specific denominational group, 10 to 12 percent of the student body. The total number of students from a variety of "charismatic" denominations (Assembly of God, Foursquare, Nazarene, Pentecostal) approximates the number of Catholic students (11 percent). Students from the "mainline" denominations (Congregational, Episcopal, Lutheran, Methodist, Presbyterian) have never reached 10 percent of the undergraduate student population. Another 7 percent of students list a variety of other denominations (including Church of Christ, Church of God, Covenant, Evangelical Free, Mormon, and other Mennonite groups).

The undergraduate student community at the college has shifted, then, from a large predominance of Mennonite Brethren to a wide variety of denominational affiliations. Most of these non-Mennonite students are evangelical in orientation, but include a significant number of Catholics and growing numbers of students who list "none" or general terms such as "non-denominational" or "protestant" as their religious preference.

All members of the college Board of Directors/Trustees were members of Mennonite Brethren churches until 1985 when openings were created for the Board to appoint its own members. Two local pastors (a Methodist and a Presbyterian) were the first non-Mennonite Brethren to be appointed to Board membership. According to the 1993 accreditation report, seven of the twenty-seven (26 percent) members of the Board (excluding student and faculty representatives) were not members of a Mennonite Brethren congregation.

All these elements—undergraduate students, faculty, and board—have become increasingly religiously diverse. But most of the college community remains Christian and, generally, evangelical in orientation. Even such broad generalizationsas these cannot be made concerning students in the Graduate and Professional Development Divisions. The college has not systematically requested information from these students concerning their religious preferences or orientation, but anecdotal evidence suggests that Mennonite Brethren make up a small percentage of students in these programs and that graduate/professional development students represent a much wider range of religious orientations than found among undergraduate students.

Gender and Ethnicity

In its early years, the college community was overwhelmingly male (except for the first three years of the Pacific Bible Institute when the student body included more females than males). As indicated in Table IV, as late as 1971 only 43 percent of the under-graduate student body, 7 percent of the full-time faculty, and no members of the Board were female.

Table IV
Percent Female by Program and Institutional Area,
for Selected Years, 1966-1993

Year	Board	Faculty	Undergrad	Fifth Year	Grad	Degree Completion
1966	0%	6%	42%	-----	-----	-----
1971	0%	7%	43%	52%	-----	-----
1976	17%	11%	49%	53%	80%	-----
1981	5%	21%	57%	80%	62%	-----
1986	8%	22%	64%	63%	73%	-----
1991	13%	24%	59%	59%	77%	62%
1993	19%	24%	61%	59%	74%	52%

By 1981 a new pattern had emerged. About 57 percent of under-graduate students, over 60 percent of graduate students, and 80 percent of teacher credential students were female. Women had joined the Board. But the faculty remained 79 percent male. A similar pattern continued in 1993 with approximately 60 percent of undergraduate and fifth-year students female while approximately three of four graduate students were female. Female representation has increased to about 20 percent in both the Board and faculty. The college's explicit affirmation in the Idea Statement of the positive value of coeducational community has been more than realized at the student level. But college leadership (faculty, board, and admin-istration) remains mostly male.

Although the college, in its Idea statement, "invites persons from various cultural, national, ethnic, and religious settings and back-grounds to participate in the educational experience," the college community remains largely racially and ethnically homogeneous, as is shown in Table V.

Table V
Undergraduate and Graduate Students
Ethnic Backgrounds

	Non-Resident Alien	Black	American Indian/ Alaskan	Asian/ Pacific Island	Hispanic	White	Total
Fall 1981							
Under-grad	11.3%	1.5%	.8%	.8%	10.8%	74.9%	398
Grad	0%	1.9%	1.0%	1.9%	.4%	93.2%	207
Fall 1986							
Under-grad	13.1%	3.8%	.9%	1.3%	14%	67%	451
Grad	.5%	2.2%	0%	2%	6.9%	88.4%	636
Fall 1991							
Under-grad	5.3%	2.4%	.2%	1.7%	10.7%	79.8%	544
Grad	.8%	2%	.9%	1.5%	8.2%	85.6%	785
Fall 1993							
Under-grad	3.8%	3.7%	.6%	4%	14.3%	73%	767
Grad	1.3%	1.9%	1.3%	2.4%	10.3%	82.4%	788

The undergraduate student body was 75 percent white in 1981, 80 percent white in 1991, and 73 percent white in 1993. The undergraduate student body has been 11 to 14 percent Hispanic during the last decade (approximately the proportion of the student body that is Catholic). Black students have been in the 2 to 4 percent range in recent years. The non-resident alien undergraduate student population has declined from 11 percent in 1981 to 4 percent in 1993.

In 1981, 93 percent of graduate students were white. That proportion declined to 82 percent in 1993. Hispanic enrollment increased from 4 percent to 10 percent during that same period. Black student enrollment remained at approximately 2 percent through the period 1981 to 1993. Small numbers of American Indian, Asian and Pacific Islander students are enrolled at both the undergraduate and graduate levels. Information concerning the ethnic background of students in the Professional Development Division is not collected.

The faculty has included one or two Hispanics and occasionally one Black member through most of the last two decades. The Board, too, has included one Hispanic member in recent years and one Black member is presently completing her first year on the Board.

The commitment to education in a coeducational environment that was affirmed in the initial Idea statement has been more than realized at the student level, but college leadership (faculty, administration, board) remains predominantly male. The college's desire to "transcend the limitations of all cultures" has been only partially realized. Non-whites remain present in the college in only small proportions compared with the population of the service area of the college.

CONCLUSIONS

The college's first fifty years have been years of both continuity and change. For more than half of these fifty years, the college's Idea statement has articulated a utopian vision for a distinctive form of educational community that is Christian, rooted in the liberal arts, and grounded in Anabaptist-Mennonite spiritual and cultural traditions. Throughout its history, the college also has affirmed its commitment to a fundamentalist-evangelical theological statement. The college, furthermore, has affirmed its openness to diversity within the community of learners that it aspires to become. During the history of the institution, its formal statements have changed in both content and function, as have the programs and people who have formed the growing and increasingly diverse community of persons who have been attracted to the institution.

"Secularization" does not provide a particularly useful interpretive perspective on these continuities and changes. A significant "secularization" has occurred in the composition of the wide variety of persons who are the recipients of the many services that the institution now provides: undergraduate residential, commuter, and degree completion programs; an intensive English language program for international students; fifth-year teacher credential programs; graduate, professional development, and curriculum development programs for educators; day care and other supportive services for the elderly; and Center for Conflict Studies and Peace-making. Like other Mennonite mission and service agencies that have not placed exclusive restrictions around the types of persons whom they will serve "in the name of Christ," the college has never drawn rigid boundaries around the community of persons whom it seeks to serve. Nor has the college required theological conformity of the many adjunct, part-time, and visiting faculty whom it employs in its attempt to deliver these services at the highest level of professional competence.

In all of its ideological self-definitions and in the persons who provide board, administrative, faculty, and staff leadership, the college remains overwhelmingly Christian in both profession and practice. An institution that is larger, offers a broader range of more specialized programs and services, provides these services to a more diverse population, and is more hierarchically and contractually organized is not necessarily more "secular." The Kingdom of God may be present in many different social and cultural forms.

The institution does struggle with ambiguities in articulating the ideological foundation upon which it seeks to maintain and extend its vision of a Christian learning community. These ambiguities concerning institutional identity and mission were a focal issue in the report of the most recent accreditation team that visited the campus in 1993.

> The team views Fresno Pacific College's most pressing problems as all stemming from a single, unresolved issue: the need to articulate a mission for the College which can unify its presently disparate components and serve as a meaningful guide for the coming decade. . . . The Team believes firmly that the College cannot afford the luxury of drifting through the next several years with a mission statement — the 1982 Fresno Pacific College Idea — that has not been refined to acknowledge its present circumstances.[16]

The college cannot resolve these issues of institutional identity and mission by returning to the Mennonite Brethren ethno-religious homogeneity that provided a strong and remarkably generous foundation for community in the early history of the institution. Neither can the college return to the single focus of undergraduate, residential, liberal arts programs and practices. Nor can the college build its identity around any single theological position — either Anabaptist-Mennonite or fundamentalist-evangelical. Internal institutional, Mennonite Brethren constituent, and environmental realities in the "markets" that the college seeks to serve with its multiple programs are too complex to allow any such simple resolution. "Better the pains of ambiguity than the pleasures of simplistic answers."[17]

The college most likely will continue to live with the ambiguities of its dual religious heritage — Anabaptist-Mennonite and fundamentalist-evangelical — and with the multiple programs and divisions that it has become. In its efforts to do so, the college might learn from persons who have already commented on relationships between Anabaptism and Evangelicalism. These include C. Norman Kraus, who focuses on differences more than similarities; John H. Redekop and Rodney Sawatsky, who emphasize commonalities more than differences; and Ronald J. Sider, who is confident that the differences can be mutually enriching for both partners in the dialogue.[18]

As the dialogue proceeds in the immediate future, several issues merit further reflection:

1. The review of institutional identity and mission, which had already begun but received added impetus from the accreditation team in 1993, should include reviews of *both* the Idea statement *and* the statement of theological orientation. The content of each should interact more directly with the realities that the institution has become. The statements should also be made more consonant with each other. Differences and similarities in the functions of the two statements should be more clearly specified. Should the college require all full-time members of the faculty and staff, for example, to identify (as presently) with the evangelical dimension of the institution, but not necessarily with the particularities of the Mennonite Brethren Confession of faith as reflected in the Idea statement? Conversely, is there a place in institutional life for full-time faculty and staff who identify with the elements of the "Anabaptist vision" included in the Idea but might not be able to affirm some specifics of the Evangelicalism that is part of the theological heritage of the Mennonite Brethren?

2. Diversity might be recognized more explicitly and positively as a source of institutional strength. The positive value of gender diversity was explicitly recognized in the affirmation, in the original Idea, that the college was a "coeducational community" ("interelationships are likely to be more realistic, and the consequent life adjustments more soundly based.") The value of diversity is acknowledged, implicitly, in the revised Idea's invitation to persons from "various cultural, national ethnic, and religious set-

tings and backgrounds to participate in the educational experience" that the college provides. But foundational to the community that the college seeks to offer, according to the Idea statement, is shared commitment to Christ and the church. The Idea does promise that the college "does not discriminate against those who cannot freely and honestly make such a commitment." But beyond this negative commitment not to discriminate, can the college affirm, in more positive terms, the contribution that might be made by persons who represent different cultural or theological traditions or even remain outside the Christian faith? Can the college affirm specific ways in which people who do not share Anabaptist-Mennonite or evangelical Christian commitment might also contribute positively to the learning experience of those who do?

3. A related issue might be the question of whether the college should specify some limits to its inclusiveness. Are there categories of persons to whom the college's invitation to community and commitment to non-discrimination does not apply? How should the boundaries and proportions of diversity differ in the various segments of the community, for example, the profiles of board, administrative, faculty or staff leadership? Of undergraduate, graduate, or professional development populations?

4. The ambiguities inherent in the nature of a Christian college are those of any religious institution. Ambiguities, dilemmas and paradoxes, by definition, permit no permanent resolution. A primary focus of campus conversations, then, should be on the nature of the processes by which institutional decisions will be made. Like the Jews at Brandeis and the Quakers at Guilford, Fresno Pacific College should work to clarify the mechanisms by which conversations between the diverse programs and cultural/religious sub-communities of the institution may be mutually enriching and fulfill the shared institutional identity and mission. Like the Jews, Quakers, and others who seek to sustain particular religious identities, the shape that these conversations assume should reflect some continuity with the specific religious heritage that the institution seeks to carry forward into the future.

To further complicate matters, these campus conversations cannot proceed in isolation from the Mennonite Brethren Conference that founded and continues to "own" the college. As suggested by the quotation at the beginning of this chapter, the future shape of the college depends not only upon internal conversations and decisions but also on the willingness and ability of both the college and the Mennonite Brethren Conference to create relationships that are mutually supportive of distinct identities and missions in the world. In 1968 Jencks and Riesman were not sanguine about the prospects for the success of such ventures. The challenges certainly have not diminished in 1995.

NOTES

1. Quoted in James Tunstead Burtchaell, "The Alienation of Christian Higher Education in America: Diagnosis and Prognosis," in *Schooling Christians: "Holy Experiments" in American Education*, ed. Stanley Hauerwas and John H. Westerhoff (Grand Rapids, Mich.: Eerdmans, 1992), 130.

2. Quoted in Ibid., 130.

3. George Marsden, "The Soul of the American University: An Historical Overview," in *The Secularization of the Academy*, ed. George Marsden and Bradley Longfield (New York: Oxford University Press, 1992), 9-45.

4. Ibid.

5. Quoted in Burtchaell, 130.

6. Thomas A. Askew, "The Shaping of Evangelical Higher Education Since World War II," in *Making Higher Education Christian: The History and Mission of Evangelical Colleges in America*, ed. Joel Carpenter and Kenneth Shipps (Grand Rapids, Mich.: Christian University Press, 1987), 137-152.

7. James Juhnke, "A Historical Look at the Development of Mennonite Higher Education in the United States," paper presented at the symposium "Mennonite Higher Education: Experience and Vision," 26-28 June 1992, Bluffton, Ohio.

8. Marsden, "The Soul," 25.

9. 43 (Winter 1993-1994): 463-487. The article contains four contributions: Marvin Fox, "Jewishness and Judaism at Brandeis University"; Michael S. Hamilton, "Fundamentalism and Education at Wheaton College"; Elizabeth B. Keiser and R. Melvin Keiser, "Quaker Principles in the Crucible of Practice"; Alice Gallin, "Catholic Higher Education Today—The Challenges of Ambiguity."

10. Ibid., 463.

11. Leland Harder, "The Quest for Equilibrium in an Established Sect" (Ph.D. diss., Northwestern University, 1962)

12. Peter M. Hamm, *Continuity and Change Among Canadian Mennonite Brethren* (Waterloo, Ont.: Wilfrid Laurier University Press, 1987).

13. Michael S. Hamilton, "Fundamentalism and Higher Education at Wheaton College," *Crosscurrents* 43 (Winter 1993-1994): 469-476.

14. Calvin Redekop, *Mennonite Society* (Baltimore: Johns Hopkins University Press, 1989), 310-311.

15. Data that are reported here have been gathered from readily accessible sources such as catalogs, accreditation reports, and summaries published by the registrars and admission offices. No attempt has been made to assure that data reported for different years are actually comparable. The size of the faculty will vary somewhat with the inclusiveness of persons listed as "faculty" in catalogs for different years, for example. Numbers of students will vary with the date used to count the student population. The wording of inquiries concerning denominational affiliation in admissions materials has also changed from year to year. The numbers reported may be read as indicative of general patterns. Other methods of data collection will be required for more precise analyses.

16. Fresno Pacific College Accreditation Report, 26-29 October 1993, 43.

17. "Living in Ambiguity," 463.

18. See, for example, *Evangelicalism and Anabaptism*, ed. C. Norman Kraus (Scottdale, Pa.: Herald Press, 1979).

Chapter 5

Singing the Christian College Song in a Mennonite Key

Paul Toews

Martin Marty, the University of Chicago historian and Lutheran churchman, in a recent address to a Lutheran hospital in Chicago, reportedly asked the question: "If you were indicted for being a Lutheran hospital would there be sufficient evidence to convict?" A version of that question ought to be asked of all Christian institutions. What is the convictable evidence that makes an institution authentically Christian? The question ought also to be asked of institutions that stand in particular theological or denominational traditions. In what ways do the distinctive elements of a denominational community and theological tradition shape the life and fabric of the institution?

Fresno Pacific College, since its inception in 1944 as Pacific Bible Institute, has existed within the contours of the larger Anabaptist-Mennonite tradition and the smaller Mennonite Brethren part of that story. Different conferences of the Mennonite Brethren Church have owned and operated the college. Every mission statement clearly links the college to the Mennonite tradition. But ownership and mission statements, important as they are, can be outward casings hiding a denominationally nondescript interior. For Fresno Pacific College to be Mennonite it must find ways of working out of and embodying essential elements of the Anabaptist-Mennonite story.

THE ANABAPTIST-MENNONITE STORY

The Mennonite story begins with the Anabaptist movement in the sixteenth century. The Anabaptists were part of the larger Reformation movement seeking change in both the theology and polity of Christendom. Anabaptists stood with Lutherans, Calvinists and other reformers in their rejection of established religious practices. They also shared with these other reformers the fundamental Christian understandings and symbols of the orthodox tradition dating back to the first century and even back to Abraham.[1] Yet they simultaneously called for additional, more radical reforms.

Historians as diverse as Ernest Troeltsch, George H. Williams, Steve Ozment, Roland Bainton, and James Stayer portray Anabaptism as a separate dissenting movement within the Protestant reformist impulse.[2] The most common label used to describe them is the "Radical Wing of the Reformation." Their fundamental break was with the medieval hope for a Christian society that encompassed everyone, or with what is commonly described as the territorial state church. The Anabaptists argued that a church linked to the coercion of the state would never be free to be the true church. They therefore sought the establishment of a church of voluntary believers, independent of civil control.

The early Anabaptist movement found followers among divergent peoples (Swiss, Dutch and Germanic), among varying social classes (peasant and learned), in diverse locations (urban and rural), and from Catholic, Lutheran and Reformed dissidents. It clearly was a pluralist and heterogeneous movement. Yet underlying this amorphous movement of radicals was a semblance of relatedness growing out of shared ecclesiological understandings.

The distinguishing marks of the separated church were to be primitivism, or the desire to restore a simple biblical pattern of life, a reading of the canon that prioritized the New Testament generally and the Sermon on the Mount particularly, biblical literalism in the interpretation of the Scriptures, adult baptism and voluntary faith in the place of infant baptism and coercive faith, a disciplined communal life, and ethical discernment within the context of the community of the faithful that included rejecting the claims of the state when they violated biblical teachings. They fully recognized that the requirements of biblical faith might not coincide with the requirements of good citizenship.

Anabaptists, troubled by the absence of any moral improvement in the Protestant territorial churches and persuaded that the ethics of coercion could not achieve that moral reformation, opted to with-draw into separate conventicles. In so choosing, they became, as Stayer wrote, "a minority hermetically separated from the fallen world and the coercion necessary for its preservation."[3] This posi-tion, in some ways, made more difficult the penetration of society and culture with religious values but it did make more possible the creation of a more purified Christian community. Furthermore it made missionizing a central activity of the church. The purified community called others to join in a declaration of personal faith and participation in the creation of this new order.

The cost of advancing these radical ideas, in the sixteenth and seventeenth centuries, was religious persecution and martyrdom. The seventeenth-century search for religious toleration and the eighteenth-century Enlightenment gave these concepts legitimacy in Western culture. But by then Mennonites and other kindred spirits were dispersed to the corners of European society where toleration was more readily secured.

The Mennonite story from the sixteenth to the nineteenth century is largely that of a people on the fringe of various social and politi-cal systems. The strong inclination to separate from worldly society and the ethical distinction between the church and the world created a bounded history marked by a high degree of cultural enclavement, political isolation and even spatial segregation.

For the forbearers of the Mennonite Brethren, who in 1944 estab-lished Pacific Bible Institute, the subsequent Mennonite story took place in the marshes of northern Germany and Prussia, the steppes of the Russian Ukraine, the North American plains frontier and the east side of California's San Joaquin Valley. These Mennonites became separated from the dominant surrounding cultures by distinctive religious commitments, language, and a distinctive cultural system. In this relative isolation they sought to build their biblical commonwealths. For centuries these Mennonites, while in many respects ideological precursors of modernity, were nourished by the social reality of an earlier time. What they built on the mar-gins of these societies were convictional communities able to medi-ate a faith increasingly lost in the radical atomization of Western culture.

Ted Regehr, a Canadian Mennonite historian, notes that Menno-nite communities around the world cite and reproduce two citations more frequently than any others.[4] They express the center of the Mennonite convictional creed. The first, a favorite of Menno Simons, the Dutch Anabaptist leader after whom Mennonites are named, is the scripture verse, "For other foundation can no man lay than that which is laid through Jesus Christ" (I. Cor. 3:11). The second statement is by Menno himself: "True evangelical faith . . . cannot lie dormant. . . . It clothes the naked; it feeds the hungry; it comforts the sorrowful, it shelters the destitute; . . . it serves those that harm it; . . . it binds up that which is wounded; . . . it has become all things to all men."[5]

The frequent juxtaposition of the two statements is not accidental. The foundation once laid in Christ, if it is a true foundation, cannot lie dormant. Things of the spirit are an important part of this foundation. Mennonites are deeply religious and devout people. They cultivate disciplines of personal piety and personal devotion. That piety can easily focus on otherworldly themes. "This world is not my home, I'm just a passing through" is easily sung by Mennonites.

Yet Mennonites are also much concerned with the things of this world. The Christian pilgrimage is a way of living in this world. It is a communal experience. It is a pilgrimage bounded by a shared covenant. The notion of an autonomous Christian, living beyond the boundary of the church with its encouragement and discipline, is foreign to Mennonite theologizing. The biblical story, as understood by Mennonites, involves individuals coming to faith in Jesus the Christ, but it is also the story of the creation of a people. It is the community of faith that signals the presence of the Kingdom of God. It does so through individuals living not primarily for themselves but for others. The communal is the context where one can experience the love and forgiveness of God. Within the collectivity of like-minded Christians one can achieve the submission and nurture of the self. Through mutual counsel, mutual discernment, and even mutual discipline the individual in community achieves both an authentic individuality and foretastes the mutuality of humankind with the Divine. The true foundation begins with the personal appropriation of God's grace but then moves on to the objective creation of a Christian community. Correct belief — orthodoxy — is important, but correct action — orthopraxis — is more important. The truth is to be embodied, to be incarnated. The incarnation of Christ — God becoming flesh, taking on human form — is what is to be imitated. Faith is a way of seeing, a way of believing, but more importantly a way of acting.

The corollaries of this understanding of faith are everywhere in Mennonite communities. One is the language of discipleship. The notion of *nachfolge*, or "following after Jesus," implies that Christians take on the task of literally exemplifying the life of Jesus. His active service to others, his peacemaking and his passion for justice become common obligations. The "kingdom of God" that he preached, while realizable only partially in this life, is what the church promotes. It is an aggressive program of personal and social reconstruction. Calvin Redekop, a Mennonite sociologist, has appropriately described the "Anabaptist vision" as containing this-worldly utopian expectations.

The witness of the church, done as Mennonite Central Committee (MCC) says, "In the Name of Christ," is sharing the good news in word and deed. The history of Mennonite missionizing activity is the story of nearly a million converts around the world. The Mennonite Brethren who founded Fresno Pacific College have always had a particularly strong commitment to world evangelization. People from many tribes, ethnicities and nations have found the Mennonite form of faith a compelling way to witness to the power of the Kingdom of God. Inhabiting differing cultural, intellectual and economic universes, all are drawn precisely because of the transforming power of a faith tradition that takes the incarnation as the starting point for personal and social reconstruction.

The impulse to offer a cup of water to the thirsty, food to the hungry and shelter to the homeless is just as strong. More Mennonites volunteer time and energy for MCC's program of international relief and development activities than for many other church activities. Their auctions and various enterprises to market third-world goods and recycle North American refuse and excess galvanize a deep Mennonite need to identify with the poor and displaced of the world.

Another corollary is the rejection of the ethics of violence. The way of discipleship includes the way of the cross. All human relationships are to be patterned after the suffering Christ who turned the other cheek rather than use the sword. The boundaries of the peaceable kingdom are to include relationships between the selves, the family, the state and all others. The way of the cross is not only the avoidance of violence but the promotion of the biblical vision of shalom. The restoration of wholeness characterized by justice, truth, respect and even love is the goal of this active peacemaking.

The practice of these corollaries of Mennonite faith often turned Mennonites into outsiders and sharpened a sense of Christian distinctiveness. It is a story of dissent, a story that stands against the standardized, conformed, established ways of the dominant culture. Heroic religious commitments have sometimes been required to maintain the tradition. Martyrology has a sacred place in Mennonite reflection. The *Martyr's Mirror*, next to the Bible, is the indispensable artifact of faith.[6] It contains the stories of some six thousand sixteenth-century Anabaptist martyrs.

But the Mennonite story is not only a heroic one. Mennonite history, like all histories, is also the story of compromise and failure. The Anabaptists and their Mennonite successors were fallible just like other Christians. If there is a perfectionist streak in Mennonite ideation, so there is also a compromised reality in Mennonite history. John Howard Yoder, the premier Mennonite social ethicist, more than twenty years ago referred to it as the gap between the "Anabaptist Vision and Mennonite Reality."[7] Whereas he called for an adjustment of reality to fit the vision, the more realistic course is to recognize the inevitable and even necessary tension or dialectic between vision and reality. It is only with an appreciation of the dialectic that institutions like Fresno Pacific College can attempt to embody the idealism of the tradition.

THE RELEVANCE OF THE MENNONITE STORY
FOR A MENNONITE COLLEGE

The predominantly young intellectuals who in the mid-1960s fashioned the Fresno Pacific Idea thought they had found in the Anabaptist-Mennonite story the elements to build a distinctive college. While the Idea was shaped by various intellectual currents, it was deeply indebted to a recovery of the Anabaptist-Mennonite story. The faculties that gathered in the early 1960s, at both the college and the adjacent Mennonite Brethren Biblical Seminary, were a new generation with a historical consciousness markedly stronger than the generation that dominated both institutions during the 1950s. They were part of a larger Mennonite Brethren recovery of its Anabaptist roots.[8] That recovery provided the primary prism through which the Idea was shaped.

The question of what in the story might be useable for the fashioning of an educational culture was not an idle one for the creators of the Idea statement. It was part of an effort to understand their own theological and historical inheritance. From the separated past it has been easy for some Mennonite institutions to emphasize that their distinctives are related to demographics. Only with a majority of Mennonite students and faculty could a distinctive Mennonite ethos be preserved.[9] The Fresno Pacific Idea explicitly rejected such boundaries and defined the Mennonite quality by reference to ideation. That did not, however, create the luxury of only etherializing about a Mennonite college. Much like the Anabaptist commitment to orthopraxis, the idea statement set in motion a search for the appropriate institutional outworking of the idea. In the decade following its articulation there were sustained attempts to translate the Idea into participatory styles of institutional governance, the practice of Christian community, creating service projects as integral to the campus life and even as a component in the academic program, and searching for the appropriate relationships between the church and its institutions and the larger culture. Those outworkings are the themes of several other essays in this volume.

Beyond the Mennonite-derived emphases covered in these other essays there are other additional academic qualities that might provide convictable evidence that Fresno Pacific is indeed an Anabaptist-Mennonite college: an intellectual disposition, an ethic and a curriculum. The disposition is the "hermeneutic of suspicion," the ethic is "transformationist," the curriculum is "reconciling."

The Hermeneutic of Suspicion

The nonconformist intellectual tradition begins with the hermeneutic of suspicion. It harbors a skepticism about reigning assumptions and practices. That is part of the generic academic enterprise. Academics are the professional demystifyers and the professional critics in any society. What Paul Ricoeur calls the "hermeneutic of suspicion" is deeply ingrained in the academic community. The task of the Christian college is not only to do that for all disciplines, but to also turn that suspicion on religious assumptions and traditions. Precisely what makes Anabaptism so attractive to many people today is the growing recognition of the cultural captivity of too much of the religious community.

The dominant religious traditions of American society seemingly have little to say to the needs of our world. While pluralism has fractured the religious groupings of the United States into innumerable entities, there clearly has been a historic liberal mainstream and a newer evangelical mainstream that have shaped much of the public dialogue on religious issues. The liberals who have held religious power for most of the twentieth century are now on the run. They are so implicated in the history of the twentieth century that they share responsibility for the dilemma in which we find ourselves. They have been edged out of power and the more reflective know they had it coming. Ostensibly evangelical presidents have occupied the White House from 1976 to 1988 and again since

1992. They have little more to show for their stewardship of the state than did the religious liberals, and their panting after power promises a seduction not much different from the liberals.

The nonconformists have historically understood that the mind is darkened and seduced by too much involvement in the existing order. One is free to hear the voice of God only when other loyalties are not strong. To hear the voice of God one must travel lightly, to be a pilgrim on the road. It is hard not to be deflected when assuming the responsibilities of Christendom and willingly take charge of society. Long before Macauley coined his famous epigram that "power corrupts and absolute power corrupts absolutely," the religious nonconformists had learned the insight. In the quest for remaining free to follow the divine imperatives Mennonites have practiced a social critique.

Only as far as Mennonite colleges continue the prophetic and innovative freedom that comes from the hermeneutic of suspicion will they continue to prosper. They will never have access to the money and facilities that allow them to compete with the conventional and established. It is precisely in questioning and pioneering that they offer promise both to themselves and to the larger academic culture. That critique, however, cannot lead to the crippling nihilism that the hermeneutic of suspicion has engendered in parts of American academe. It must be directed toward reconstruction and transformation.

A Transformationist Ethic

Long ago, G. K. Chesterton, the British observer of America, noted that America is a nation with the soul of a church. But then he added that America also has churches with the soul of a nation. What Chesterton and others suggest is that the vaunted separation of church and state, in this culture, did not sunder the Constantinian tradition. Paradoxically it created a neo-Constantinian arrangement that while more providing a kind of institutional religious freedom may have created a more damaging theological bondage.[10]

At the heart of the neo-Constantinian tradition was the project that Stanley Hauerwas and William Willimon describe as "seeking to make the gospel credible to the modern world."[11] It is that quest that has made the church's theology, for centuries, predominantly apologetic. Faced with what the German philosopher Lessing called the "ugly wide ditch" of history that separated the ancient faith from modern science, the church has been trying to develop a modern world view, trying to escape its pre-scientific world view. Schleier-macher's hope of making the faith credible to Christianity's "cultural despisers" has been much of the agenda of this apologetic tradition. And so theology has been concerned to translate the ancient faith into the categories of existentialism, Whiteheadian process theology, psychoanalysis, or Marxist analysis to render it believable.

The degree to which American evangelicals have wedded themselves to enlightenment science is well documented by many observers. Mark Noll, the Wheaton historian, terms it the "scandal of the Evangelical mind." Both knowingly and unknowingly evangelicals in their search for cultural relevance sought to translate their ideas into forms acceptable to enlightenment understandings. Because of this process the explicit task of theologizing and the implicit role of the church in the society became largely acculturated to the dominant cultural values.[12]

From the stance of the Radical Reformation this entire venture is misguided. The theology of translation assumes that there is some "kernel of real Christianity, some abstract essence" that can be preserved and integrated into changing scientific world views. The Mennonite approach to faith begins at a different place. As Stanley Hauerwas and William H. Willimon write, "in Jesus we meet not a presentation of basic ideas about God, the world and humanity, but an invitation to join up, to become part of the movement," to become part of the new people. Our witness is the earthly imitation of the Kingdom.[13]

The theological enterprise of integration or accommodation runs through both liberal and evangelical theologizing. Christian colleges have been preoccupied with this theological apologetical tradition. Much of the concern for the integration of faith, culture, and learning has been part of this apologetic tradition. By finding the points of congruence they entertained the hope that we might be able to Christianize the culture. Integration is a limited and perhaps even an inadequate metaphor for Mennonites to use. Transformationist language is a more adequate descriptor of the intended relationship of faith to knowledge, of faith to culture. Integration has become too closely identified with the Constantinian tradition. Like so much of that tradition it has meant the absorption of faith into the cultural system.

A Mennonite college should be concerned that students appropriate high culture (the works of natural science, philosophy, theology, music, painting, poetry, architecture and all the rest that comprises a liberal arts curriculum) as enriching for faith. But it also must have another calling. That is to utilize knowledge and commitment in the fashioning of alternative Christian communities. That task does not discount the importance of learning, but it does redirect it.

A Reconciling Curriculum

The central theme of the gospels is the reconciling of humankind to God. But in becoming reconciled to God, we are also to become reconciled to each other, to nature, to the neighbor, to the stranger, and even to the enemy.

Whatever the twentieth century is, it is not the century apt to win the Nobel Peace Prize. It has been an era of accelerating violence: person against person, person against family, tribe against tribe, ideology against ideology, nation against nation, and religion against religion. Overriding the many localized conflicts has been an unparalleled nuclear arms race and the threat of global suicide.

A Mennonite college true to its heritage will direct learning toward themes of reconciliation. It will make active peacemaking, conflict resolution and reconciliation a centerpiece of the curriculum. Colleges in the Mennonite tradition ought to excel at unmasking the structures of injustice, the dispositions and values that generate destructive violence. Learning the techniques of conflict resolution and peacemaking should be central to every student's experience. One of our tasks is to provide a pacifist alternative to this fundamental crisis of our times.

Nicholas Wolterstorff, a philosopher of the Reformed tradition, has argued that Christian colleges in the latter part of the twentieth century must respond to the needs of a suffering humanity. Acquiring the requisite piety, skills of evangelism and insight into the high culture have been noble commitments that organized Christian colleges in the past. But with a world in need of "re-formation," new tasks of active intervention are waiting. The task of simply imparting a Christian world view is a luxury of the past. Christian education, Wolterstorff argues, needs to "equip and motivate students for a Christian way of being and acting in the world."[14] What a Mennonite college imparts should be a way of acting and being that includes compassion, justice and reconciliation.

THE MENNONITE DIALECTIC AT FRESNO PACIFIC COLLEGE

The fifty years of Fresno Pacific's history coincide with a period of unusual stress and change for the Mennonite Brethren people. Still largely encased in the 1940s in their small rural communities, they perpetuated distinctive cultural and theological understandings. They were what sociologists call an "ethno-religious" group—a cross between a religious community and an ethnic group.

Today the Mennonite Brethren can hardly be thought of as outsiders. The story of persecution and isolation is increasingly a foreign past. The Mennonite Brethren are now the most educated and urbanized among all of the Mennonite groups.[15] They freely participate in the central institutions of American society. In many ways they have sociologically made their peace with modernity. They feel at home in American society. There is very little sense of "over-againstness" among the Mennonite Brethren. They mix freely in Rotary clubs, at local Chamber of Commerce functions, at Republican fund-raisers, and in the National Association of Evangelicals. While they continue to nurture the distinctive elements of the Anabaptist inheritance they are also among some of the most ecumenical Mennonites. A long history of cooperation with Baptists (particularly German Baptists and their descendants), the Christian and Missionary Alliance and other conservative protestant bodies indicates a willingness to make common cause with other evangelical groups.

The Mennonite Brethren ease of associating with different traditions goes back to the 1860 beginnings of the movement in south Russia. Present at the Mennonite Brethren birth was a theological pluralism that included Pietism, European Evangelicalism and Anabaptism. The result has been a tradition containing within itself diverse—and perhaps even contradictory—currents. Differing parts of the Mennonite Brethren world have accentuated and diminished various elements of the inheritance. Among the United States Mennonite Brethren generally, and particularly among those on the West Coast, time and social movement had dimmed the Anabaptist part of their religious inheritance. During the last fifty years the pressures for assimilation into American ways, the increasing desire not to be different and the entry into the broader American middle class pruned away many of the distinguishing qualities of earlier Mennonite Brethren. In the transition it has been easy to confuse the ethnic and the religious. After all, other Christians did not hold dear the same things, so those distinctive elements could easily be put into the category of cultural trappings or ethnic remnants.

Thus, when an Anabaptist renaissance occurred during the 1960s at both the college and the adjacent Mennonite Brethren Biblical Seminary, it could be understood by some Mennonite Brethren not as the recovery of a partially lost tradition but as a foreign import. Furthermore, coming just when some Mennonite Brethren were pleased with the loss of the cultural boundaries that had fenced them off from American society, here was a young faculty offering a new set of ideological boundaries to again impede an easy association with American culture. While the revival of Mennonite history might bring nostalgic memories, the revival of Anabaptist theology challenged the acculturation process with its embrace of the American order. To some parts of the church, this neo-Anabaptism seemed like the resurfacing of older sectarian curbs.

Others in the church found this neo-Anabaptism unacceptable because it seemed like a disguised secularity. Its categories were too political. The mystical Jesus of Pietism was replaced by a more political Jesus. For Mennonite Brethren influenced by Pietism, ethics had been thought of almost exclusively in personal terms. Corporate ethics, in the sense that there are collective signs of the kingdom that organize the political and social behavior of God's people, were a casualty of this kind of ethical Pietism. When the young college faculty called on itself and the church to be transformationist and prophetic it could easily sound to some like the political and cultural critique of the 1960s. The hermeneutic of suspicion is not advantageous to a people entering the dominant culture, and a transformationist gospel is not suited to settling in and being peaceable people in a militaristic society.

That a Mennonite Brethren college would feel in a particular way the tensions of the Mennonite Brethren story is altogether appropriate. Colleges, when they do their task, always stand on the margins between religious peoples and the larger world. That is particularly so for colleges of religious peoples with a definable cultural tradition. They historically face both inward toward the small Mennonite village and outward toward the larger society. Mediating the dialectic of acceptance and suspicion, of embrace and distancing between the smaller religious community and the larger world is part of the task of a denominational college in the Anabaptist tradition.

History has a way of playing tricks. For over 470 years people have been singing the Mennonite song. For most of those years it has been sung on the margins of Christendom. For many the song has sounded like a dissonant chord. But the story of God's people, like the biblical logic, is an ironic one: the hidden becomes visible, the last become first, and the meek inherit the earth. So also it is for the Mennonite story: the marginal becomes central, the minor chords become major, the dissonant becomes harmonic.

One need not look very far today to witness the embrace of Mennonites. In ecumenical discussions the eye drift is increasingly to the Mennonite participants. Rankings of small colleges regularly include Mennonite colleges, including Fresno Pacific, as among the best in the nation. Mennonite Central Committee and Mennonite Mental Health services are regularly ranked as among the best providers in their respective fields. The Anabaptist-Mennonite story is that of a small and marginal people. But Anabaptist-Mennonite ideation is open to all who embrace it. It contains the possibilities for shaping a college that is biblically faithful, intellectually critical and expansive, culturally pluralistic, ethically transformative and morally distinctive. A Christian college singing in the Mennonite key can indeed offer a distinctive melody to American higher education.

NOTES

1. See Walter Klaassen, "The Quest for Anabaptist Identity," in *Anabaptist-Mennonite Identities in Ferment*, Leo Driedger and Leland Harder eds., Occasional Papers, number 14 (Elkhart, Ind.: Institute of Mennonite Studies, 1990), 16-17, for a discussion of the importance of Mennonites understanding their history and inheritance dating back to the beginnings of the Judaic-Christian story instead of looking only to the sixteenth century.

2. See Ernst Troeltsch, *Protestantism and Progress: A Historical Study of the Relationship of Protestantism to the Modern World*, trans. W. Montgomery (Boston: Beacon Press, 1956); George H. Williams, *The Radical Reformation* (Philadelphia: The Westminster Press, 1962); Steven Ozment, *The Age of Reform, 1550-1650: An Intellectual and Religious History of Late Medieval and Reformation Europe* (New Haven: Yale University Press, 1980); Roland H. Bainton, *The Reformation of the Sixteenth Century* (Boston: Beacon Press, 1952); James M. Stayer, *Anabaptists and the Sword* (Lawrence, Kansas: Coronado Press, 1972).

3. Stayer, 330.

4. Unpublished manuscript on Mennonites in Canada, 1940-1970.

5. *The Complete Writings of Menno Simons, c. 1496-1561*, trans. Leonard Verduin, ed. J. C. Wenger (Scottdale, Pa.: Herald Press, 1956), 307.

6. Tieleman Jansz van Braght, an elder in the Mennonite congregation of Dordrecht, The Netherlands, published in 1660 a work in Dutch that in English is usually called the *Martyr's Mirror*. Since its original publication it has been reproduced countless times in Dutch, German and English translations and editions.

7. John Howard Yoder, "Anabaptist Vision and Mennonite Reality," in *Consultation on Anabaptist Mennonite Theology*, ed. A. J. Klassen (Fresno, Calif.: Council of Mennonite Seminaries, 1970), 1-46.

8. I have tried to sketch the outlines of that recovery in "Differing Historical Imaginations and the Changing Identity of the Mennonite Brethren," in *Anabaptism Revisited: Essays on Anabaptist-Mennonite Studies in Honor of C. J. Dyck*, ed. Walter Klaassen (Scottdale, Pa.: Herald Press, 1992).

9. Among the Mennonite liberal arts colleges, Fresno Pacific College and Bluffton College have traditionally had the smallest percentage of Mennonite student bodies. For some years in both schools less than twenty-five percent have been Mennonite. The other institutions—Bethel, Tabor, Goshen, Eastern Mennonite and Hesston—have had a considerably higher percentage of Mennonite students. The schools under the Mennonite Church's Board of Higher Education—Goshen, Eastern Mennonite and Hesston—have for decades operated under guidelines that required Mennonite students to be a majority of the student body.

10. Quoted in Sidney E. Mead, *The Nation With the Soul of a Church* (New York: Harper and Row, 1975), 48. See also Mead, *The Lively Experiment: The Shaping of Christianity in America* (New York: Harper and Row, 1963). The two books offer a brilliant interpretation of the relationship between Christianity and American culture.

11. This entire paragraph draws on Stanley Hauerwas and William Willimon, *Resident Aliens: Life in the Christian Colony* (Nashville: Abingdon Press, 1989), chapter 7. The quote is from page 19.

12. Mark A. Noll, *The Scandal of the Evangelical Mind* (Grand Rapids, Mich.: William B. Eerdmans, 1994).

13. Hauerwas and Willimon, *Resident Aliens*, 21.

14. Nicholas Wolterstorff, "The Mission of the Christian College at the End of the Twentieth Century," *Faculty Dialog* (Fall 1984): 47.

15. See J. Howard Kauffman and Leo Driedger, *The Mennonite Mosaic: Identity and Modernization* (Scottdale, Pa.: Herald Press, 1991) for a comparative study of four Mennonite denominations and the Brethren in Christ.

Chapter 6

"Fresno Pacific College is a Prophetic College"

Dalton Reimer

"Where there is no prophecy, the people cast off restraint."
(Proverbs 29:18, NRSV)[1]

The vision of Pacific as a prophetic college was set forth in one of the seven major sections of the original Idea of 1966. This section has had a mixed history. When the Idea was first published in the 1969-1970 college catalog, this section, together with the section identifying the college as an "experimental college," was deleted. The full Idea appeared in the college catalog for the first time in 1972. When the Idea was revised in 1982, no reference to Fresno Pacific as a prophetic college appeared at all. It again appears in the 1994 revision.

In the words of the original statement,

Pacific College is a Prophetic College. The college views itself as a center of independent critique of all of men's endeavors. It is not simply an institution that transmits the values of the culture in which it exists. It purposes to serve as the conscience of society and the church rather than become a tool of any institution or idealism.

Cultural critique was pervasive in American society during the 1960s. The civil rights movement, the Vietnam conflict, and politics intensified by assassinations and distrust of established authorities dominated the consciousness of the nation. Countercultural movements of all sorts emerged. To declare oneself as "prophetic" in this context was to be both "with it" and suspect. Among conservatives supporting the college, suspicion was more likely. The inclusion of this segment in the Pacific Idea, however, was not centrally motivated by the spirit of the time; rather, it was motivated by a deep consciousness of the college's longer Anabaptist Christian heritage. Prophetic witness to the unity of faith and practice in obedience to God, though religious or worldly powers may oppose and even persecute, has been a hallmark of this tradition.

THE PROPHETIC ORIENTATION

The prophet Micah succinctly summarized the message of the biblical prophets: "What does the Lord require of you but to do justice, and to love kindness, and to walk humbly with your God?" (Micah 6:8). As Old Testament scholar Bernhard W. Anderson has observed,

> Just as rabbis summed up the whole Torah in the two great commandments "You shall love the Lord your God with all your heart, and with all your soul, and with all your strength, and with all your mind and your neighbor as yourself" (Luke 10:27; Deuteronomy 6:5; Leviticus 19:18), so [Micah's] pithy passage encompasses the major themes of the prophetic message: "Let justice roll down like waters" (Amos 5:24); "I [God] desire mercy, not sacrifice" (Hosea 6:6); when the Day of the Lord comes, the pride of people will be humbled (Isaiah 2:8-11).[2]

In the New Testament the apostle and prophet Paul summarized the prophetic message: "Do not be conformed to this world, but be transformed by the renewing of your minds, so that you may discern what is the will of God — what is good and acceptable and perfect" (Romans 12:2). Phillips renders this passage: "Don't let the world around you squeeze you into its own mould, but let God re-make you so that your whole attitude of mind is changed." In his second letter to the church in Corinth, the apostle Paul speaks of persons being changed or "metamorphosed" into the likeness of Christ (II Corinthians 3:18). The prophetic challenge, then, is not to be conformed to the world, but to be transformed into the image of Christ. "The task of prophetic ministry," Walter Brueggemann writes in *The Prophetic Imagination*, "is to nurture, nourish, and evoke a consciousness and perception alternative to the consciousness and perception of the dominant culture around us."[3]

The pressure to conform to the world is pervasive and unending. Ancient Israel was forever seduced by the practices and gods of their neighbors. The prophets railed against this conformity. They denounced it as spiritual prostitution, and pointed the people back to God as their true love. But ancient Israel was not alone. Every age faces this pressure. Brueggemann observes that "prophetic ministry has to do not primarily with addressing specific public crises but with addressing, in season and out of season, the dominant crisis that is enduring and resilient, of having our alternative vocation co-opted and domesticated."[4]

Christian higher education itself has experienced this domestication in American society. In 1960 Yale historian Sydney Ahlstrom observed that a key fact of American higher education is that in the last several centuries it has been "remorselessly secularized."[5] No institution is immune. Pressures come from various quarters. Consider, for example, the fact that faculty for Christian colleges are educated principally in the graduate programs of secular universities. Here they are acculturated into the dominant secular perspectives of their disciplines, which routinely become themes of their later teaching in a Christian college. Furthermore, textbooks used in classrooms throughout Christian higher education tend to be the prevailing secular texts of the time. This is not to argue for a narrowing of attention to the scholarship of the world, but simply to recognize the frequent provincialism of this scholarship in its neglect of religious perspectives. Furthermore, accreditation agencies move institutions toward the prevailing norms of the larger academic culture. So pressures toward conformity are multitudinous. The Christian response should not be a cloistered education. On the contrary, the Christian college should actively and rigorously engage the world. Indeed, a prophetic college will invite and promote this engagement. But it does mean that the Christian college will not receive much help from the larger academic culture. If it is to be prophetic, the Christian college will need to be so intentionally and deliberately.

To be a prophetic college requires that an institution first order its own house. This begins with a clear articulation of its center. In this respect the formation of the Pacific Idea in the mid-1960s was a prophetic act. Prophets have a center. A prophetic college is one that has united around a particular core of value and has chosen actively to educate from the perspective of that core. The prophet has a stance, a point-of-view. Transformation as process is not an end in itself, but is directed toward clear goals.

To be a prophetic college, furthermore, requires the continuing education and nurture of that center with the faculty, administration and staff. Given the domination of the secular university in graduate education, a Christian college must take upon itself the responsibility to re-educate faculty, administrators and staff who join its community. One must enter a prophetic college first as a learner.

To be a prophetic college, finally, requires prophetic teaching. Prophetic teaching unites word and deed. This unity is central to the Anabaptist understanding of New Testament Christianity. Thus faculty and leaders in a prophetic college will not only talk about integrity, but will also practice integrity. They will not only talk about community, but will also create community. They will not only talk about responsible investments, but will also practice responsible investments. They will not only talk about peace, but will also be peacemakers.

In 1980 Bethel College, a Mennonite college in North Newton, Kansas, sponsored a National Conference on Faith and Learning. Church historian Martin E. Marty, a speaker at the conference, later reflected on the experience in a *Christian Century* article entitled "On 'Being Prophetic.'" He observed that at the conference participants frequently called upon their Anabaptist peers "to be prophetic in America." In a perceptive critique of this call, he observed:

> Today prophecy comes to mean radical criticism of society. That is cheap. Stick around; on glum days even I can provide that — at no expense, including none to myself. The tongue screws may be out there in the future, but they are not out there in the current landscape. Should the heirs of radical Protestantism prove they have prophetic credentials by being more shrill, publishing more statistics about injustice, or having a bad conscience for not being more strident? Again, I wonder.
>
> Or could it be that today the critical and prophetic burden should pass also to others, while the Mennonites keep doing what they do at their best? Praising God in song and art and prose, simply. Loving the soil and helping bring forth its fruit. Being among the first with almost the most to meet boat people or share know-how or grain. Sending a large percentage of their young into service occupations. Providing alternative service. Maybe all those things, subtle though they be, will take more doing and will speak more clearly than would "being prophetic." I think to do these things would *be* "being prophetic."[6]

A prophetic college unites word and deed, but in the end may witness most powerfully through demonstrations of what it proclaims. A college that has ordered its own house by articulating its faith center, by first educating its own faculty, administrators and staff, and by uniting faith and practice in its teaching strategy, is prepared to be a prophetic college for its students and for the world.

This ordering of Fresno Pacific's own house over the years has been imperfect. The Idea itself has at times received considerable attention; at others times it has receded into the background. The education of the faculty, administrators and staff to the college's center has been very uneven. Faith and practice have at times been united and at other times been contradictory. But through it all the Idea has endured as the vision toward which the college continues to grow.

FAITH AND CULTURE

The relationship between faith and culture has been a key concern in prophetic history. Since the 1950s the discussion of this relationship often has been shaped by H. Richard Niebuhr's seminal work, *Christ and Culture.*[7] Niebuhr identifies five different views of the relationship between faith and culture in historic Christianity. The categories "Christ against culture" and the "Christ of culture" represent the extremes of Niebuhr's continuum. The first sees Christ as opposed to culture, the second sees Christ as integrated with culture. Between these extremes are three more central positions: "Christ above culture," "Christ and culture in paradox," and "Christ the transformer of culture." The "Christ above culture" view is exemplified by the synthesis of natural law and the higher way of Jesus in Medieval culture. "Christ and culture in paradox" suggests that Christ represents a higher way, but reality dictates that humans must also adjust to the ways of the world to be productive citizens. Christ as transformer suggests the view that Christ is both independent of culture and a shaper of culture.

Niebuhr linked the Anabaptists with the "Christ against culture" view, but that interpretation has been strongly challenged. Charles Scriven, for example, has argued that the Anabaptists represent a more adequate understanding of the transformative perspective, which Niebuhr favors, than does Niebuhr himself. Indeed, Scriven asserts that "the true Niebuhrian way is the Anabaptist way."[8]

The Fresno Pacific Idea envisions the college to be a transforming presence in the church and world. As stated in the original version, the college "purposes to serve as the conscience of society and the church." These are strong words and may even sound presumptuous, but they suggest the deep feeling of the framers of the Idea that the college should have a strong, prophetic witness. The further assertion that the college "views itself as a center of independent critique" and not "a tool of any institution or idealism" should not be understood as rejecting identification with the church or culture. Independence and identification may seem contradictory, but can coexist in a creative tension. Niebuhr's view of Christ as transformer of culture suggests both. Those who proclaim the bumper sticker message, "love it or leave it," would quickly resolve this tension by separation. But for the prophet, independence and identification are handmaidens. The biblical prophets were most often participant critics in their communities. They were members of the community and identified deeply with the community. They were willing to risk their very lives because they cared so deeply on one hand about truth and justice, and on the other about the community.

THE PERSONA OF THE PROPHET

Eyes and Ears

Biblical prophets were first called Seers. They were in close communion with God and gifted with keen insight into the human condition of their times. Discerning eyes and ears are prerequisites for prophecy.

True prophets are not driven by self-interest or self-seeking. Their pursuit is truth and righteousness. Viktor E. Frankl has wisely observed: "The ability of the eye to see is dependent upon its inability to see itself."[9] Likewise, the ability of the ear to hear is dependent upon its inability to hear itself. True prophets have clear vision and hearing focused on God's will for creation and humankind.

Memory

The prophet is a storyteller. The prophet remembers God and the story of God's people. To pursue strange gods is to forget God and God's shaping of one's own unique story. The prophets reminded Israel of God's call and promise to Abraham, their sojourn in Egypt, deliverance from Egypt, struggles in the wilderness, and entry into the promised land. Faith is rooted in history. Remembering God's shaping presence in the past is a key to renewal in the present.

God provided ancient Israel with aids to remember pivotal moments of their history. The people were to celebrate the Passover to keep alive the memory of their liberation from Egypt. They erected monuments of stones to keep alive the memory of such events as the miraculous crossing of the Jordan into the promised land. Yet ancient Israel, as people today, forgot. The prophet was God's instrument to call the people back to memory.

No one has made the case for remembering more poignantly in our time than the Jewish writer and prophet Elie Wiesel. As a survivor of the Holocaust, Wiesel has determined that this and future generations must never forget what happened. Elhanan, a character in Wiesel's novel, *The Forgotten*, states Wiesel's case well. Elhanan, too, is a survivor of the camps, and in his old age is losing his memory. He offers a prayer to God about remembering. Wiesel calls it simply "Elhanan's Prayer":

> You well know, You, source of all memory, that to forget is to abandon, to forget is to repudiate. . . . Remember, God of history, that You created man to remember. You put me into the world, You spared me in time of danger and death, that I might testify. What sort of witness would I be without my memory?[10]

Witness requires memory, but prophets must do more than remember their own stories. Prophets must also understand other stories. Prophets live at the interface between faith and culture in all of its manifestations, including politics, economics, business, human relations, education and the arts. The stories of these human enterprises must also be understood if prophets are to speak with insight.

Voice

"If I have prophetic powers," the apostle Paul writes, "but do not have love [*agape*], I am nothing" (I Corinthians 13:2). Prophets who speak truth without love are like "a noisy gong or a clanging cymbal" (I Corinthians 13:1). They make much noise, but their message does not take root.

The biblical prophets adapted the tone in which they spoke to the situation. Jesus as prophet demonstrates the possibilities. The gentle but firm Jesus is revealed on the Samaritan road discoursing across cultural, religious and gender barriers to the Samaritan woman at Jacob's historic well. Jesus gently confronted the woman with the truth of her situation, and she recognized him as prophet (John 4).

The gentle but firm Jesus is further revealed on the Jericho road calling chief tax collector Zacchaeus down from his bleacher seat in the sycamore tree and inviting himself to his home. We do not know what Jesus said to him in his house, but Zacchaeus' declaration-"Look, half of my possessions, Lord, I will give to the poor; and if I have defrauded anyone of anything, I will pay back four times as much"-indicates that whatever Jesus said took hold (Luke 19:8).

Jesus often used this gentle, yet clearly confrontational, mode with those who were oppressed and authentic searchers for truth. Both the Samaritan woman and Zacchaeus manifested lifestyles contrary to the way of Jesus, but both were confronted and drawn to faith in a straightforward but gentle mode. One could multiply the examples of this mode from the life of Jesus as he addressed those across the social and economic structures of the society in which he moved.

A second mode was more pointed. Harsh words of critique in the more stereotypical image of the flaming prophet were reserved for those who were self-righteous and resistant to faith. The stubborn scribes and Pharisees as well as the resistant cities of Chorazin, Bethsaida and Capernaum are illustrative. On these Jesus pronounced harsh words of judgment (Matthew 23:13-39; 11:20-24).

Strong words were also addressed by Jesus to those who followed him but for the wrong reasons. His prophetic challenge to those who chose to follow him after he fed the five thousand in the wilderness, simply because they thought he would be a continuing source for easy food, led to a mass disaffection. So many turned and left when confronted with his hard truth that he finally turned to his core group of twelve disciples and asked whether they too wished to leave (John 6). For the prophet, right reasons for actions are important. Crowds hold no virtue if they are attracted for the wrong reasons. The prophet's strength rests in the ability to speak the truth though the crowds may vanish. The demagogue speaks what the crowd wishes to hear, the prophet what they need to hear. Jesus was a prophet.

A prophet who escalates a confrontation to strong words must not forsake *agape* love. When a Samaritan village would not receive Jesus on one of his journeys through Samaria to Jerusalem, James and John, those sons of fisherman Zebedee whom Jesus renamed "Sons of Thunder," lived up to their nickname by asking whether they should call down fire from heaven to consume the village (Luke 9:51-56). Jesus rebuked them. The intent of the prophet is not to destroy, but to convert the other. Truth speaking may require a hard message, but the message must be delivered with the intent to effect change and not destroy. There is a place for "tough love," and the goal is conversion.

Hands and Feet

Finally, true prophets are persons of action who model what they preach. Here we may return to the insight of Martin E. Marty about "being prophetic." Actions in the end may be more prophetic than words. The image of the flaming prophet making pronouncements from some high or bully pulpit is a stereotype. Prophecy is not bound to a single form, but in the end is most powerful when modeled in action.

A PROPHETIC COLLEGE

In the first chorus from "The Rock," poet and prophet T. S. Eliot reflects on the cycles of nature and history. He climaxes the opening stanza of the chorus with a series of questions and a conclusion:

Where is the Life we have lost in living?
Where is the wisdom we have lost in knowledge?
Where is the knowledge we have lost in information?
The cycles of Heaven in twenty centuries
Bring us farther from God and nearer to the Dust.[11]

A prophetic college is not content simply to transmit the accumulated knowledge of the past to the present generation. It is possible, as Harvard professor Robert Coles has observed, for a student to earn an "A" in a course on religion or moral development and yet flunk life itself.[12] A prophetic college calls itself, its students and its constituencies to account for the totality of being. Education in this mode cannot be simply the cultivation of the mind; it must be the transformation of the whole person. A college accomplishes such an education through its teaching and mentoring, curriculum, convocations and worship, student life programs, public service programs, and the example of its faculty, administrators and staff. Fresno Pacific College has pursued these goals in several ways.

Teaching and Mentoring

New undergraduates at Fresno Pacific, whether first-year students or transfers, begin their educational experience by taking a biblical studies course called "Jesus and the Christian Community." Central to this course are the Gospel texts. An additional text used in the 1990s has been Donald B. Kraybill's *The Upside Down Kingdom*.[13] Kraybill's work illuminates the radical nature of God's Kingdom as articulated in the Gospels, and demonstrates now the values of this Kingdom often oppose the values promoted in the prevailing culture. This is prophetic teaching.

The first-year version of "Jesus and the Christian Community" is taught by faculty members from across the academic disciplines of the college. This course becomes a means of engaging issues pertaining to the fundamental values and shape of God's Kingdom. These faculty also serve as mentors to first-year students in small groups called collegiums. They are assisted by student mentor assistants who have previously completed the course. A service project and a weekend mountain retreat add experiential components to the course, and provide demonstrations of Christian values.

Graduate students in the college's master's program in education encounter similar ideas in "Values in School and Society." This course includes an examination of the implications of the college's distinctive orientation expressed in the Idea and its related graduate mission statement for schools and society.

Prophetic teaching occurs in varying degrees throughout the college. A student who took course work concurrently in a public institution and at Fresno Pacific observed that in the public institution, she had learned to do what needed to be done as a participating member of a particular profession. Basic values undergirding the profession, however, were not questioned. At Fresno Pacific, she reported students not only learned how to do things, but also to question and examine basic values. Surely such questioning may occur in either place, but a prophetic college is committed to such questioning as a critical part of its mission.

Curriculum

Curricular structures also enhance the prophetic ministry of the college. For example, the faculty in the early 1990s adopted the "Focus Series" within the General Education program. These are six to eight-unit interdisciplinary concentrations that unite biblical/theological and interdisciplinary studies. Focus Series themes reflect central concerns of the college, such as Anabaptist-Mennonite Studies, Environmental Studies, Intercultural Studies, and Studies in Conflict and Peacemaking. Students select one as part of their General Education program. Each series challenges existing understandings and practices in both the church and world.

Convocations and Worship

College Hour is the college's designation for its twice-weekly convocation and worship gatherings. A long tradition exists of including in this series speakers and storytellers who have challenged the prevailing culture and modeled alternatives based on a commitment to Christian discipleship. Themes such as discipleship, service, justice, culture, peace and ministry are common in College Hour.

Student Life Programs

Community, service, and "servant leadership" are dominant themes of student life programs at Fresno Pacific. These themes are expressed in a variety of programs including residential life, student leadership development, and service ministry. Theory and practice are united in these programs to build alternative models to individualism, the focus on self-seeking and advancement, and a power-oriented concept of leadership.

The boundary between academic and student life at Fresno Pacific is soft. At times the boundary is indecipherable. Community emerges in classrooms, faculty become counselors, and students help and serve each other both in the classroom and beyond it. Program structures such as those in the adult degree completion program encourage integration. Here students progress through their entire program in a single learning group that becomes an intentional community. Graduate programs develop their own unique dynamics and sub-communities. The focus of the college Idea on the holistic development of persons encourages faculty, administrators and staff to relate to students in multiple ways beyond the narrow specifications of a particular work assignment. Interpersonal interaction is encouraged through a de-emphasis on the use of formal academic titles and the general practice of calling persons by their first names, including faculty.

Public Service Programs

The Older Adult Social Service program, or OASIS, is a college program that provides alternative day care for semi-dependent elderly persons. This program integrates service and learning for students, and serves as a model of ministry in an area of need not addressed by the usual social agencies of society. It is an example of *being* prophetic in the world. The college's Center for Conflict Studies and Peacemaking provides training, consultation and mediation services for persons and organizations within the church, school and community. In the midst of a culture torn by conflict and violence, "peace" is a prophetic word. A prophetic college will build alternative models of public service as it bears witness to the community in which it exists.

Example and Model

In the end perhaps the most powerful witness of the prophet comes through modeling, personally and communally. Prophets witness not only through speaking, but also through demonstrating. Charles Scriven speaks of being a "transformative example."[14] A college that seeks to be prophetic must first model what it professes. Faculty, administrators and staff must model in their own persons what they profess. The college in its corporate existence must model Christian community. Otherwise, a college becomes guilty of the heresy that Jesus observed in the first-century scribes and pharisees. Simply put, Jesus said, "they do not practice what they preach" (Matthew 23:3). Hence, their witness was ineffective if not destructive, and they are not to be emulated.

Faculty in American higher education have been characterized as "invisible models." Most of their lives are closed or not known by the students they teach. Fresno Pacific has taken steps to encourage more visibility. Beyond the sharing that occurs in the classroom, faculty are given financial support to entertain students in their homes and to take students out for lunch. A long-standing tradition is for one or two faculty each term to share their personal stories with the undergraduate student body in the College Hour program. Students have consistently rated these among the highest valued College Hours. Surveys of students and alumni at Fresno Pacific reveal that student-faculty relationships are among the most valued aspects of a Fresno Pacific education. The power of example and modeling is inestimable.

Modeling is also a matter of corporate life. Jesus once told his followers: "By this everyone will know that you are my disciples, if you have love for one another" (John 13:35). Communities in the Jesus way are called to be model communities in the world.

Community has been a central tenet of the Fresno Pacific Idea. Throughout the years the college has sought to realize what it means to be a community in the Jesus way. Community transcends national, cultural and ethnic boundaries. Community has meant practicing redemptive discipline among its members. The college has sought to be a community where people support each other. Collaborative and consensual decision making has been the ideal, though not always realized. Members of the community have sought to work out conflicts in cooperative and restorative ways, though often imperfectly. The college has worked at developing an approach to leadership often called "servant leadership."

Model building should be a continuing and active pursuit of a Christian prophetic college. Experimenting and demonstrating how the communities of the church and world can become genuine communities of *Shalom* should be a central mission of such a college.

CONCLUSION

Scholars have debated whether the gift of prophecy as understood in the New Testament church has survived that period. Does God still give his people the gift of prophecy as in that time? Whether so or not, the framers of the Fresno Pacific Idea of the 1960s were convinced that a Christian college must be prophetic if it is to accomplish its mission of serving the church and world. This conviction has now been reaffirmed in the 1994 revision. Realistically, such a prophetic stance may be accomplished rarely through a direct word from God as received by biblical prophets. Nevertheless, God has revealed himself through Christ, and the prophetic foundation for examining the life of the church and world has been established. Michael Novak has observed that on occasion God breaks into human existence in a marvelous, revelatory way analogous to the "flight of the dove." More often, however, humans are faced with the hard work of discovering truth analogous to the "ascent of the mountain."[15] A prophetic teacher and a prophetic college must be committed to this hard work, while also being grateful for those unexpected moments when God breaks through and illuminates life in a special and unique way. But it will be mostly the hard work of climbing the mountain that will qualify the teacher and college to speak and act prophetically.

NOTES

1. All scripture quotations are taken from the New Revised Standard Version.

2. Bernhard W. Anderson, "What Does God Require of Us?" *Bible Review* 11 (February 1995): 19.

3. Walter Brueggemann, *The Prophetic Imagination* (Philadelphia: Fortress Press, 1978), 13.

4. Ibid., 13.

5. Sydney E. Ahlstrom, "Toward the Idea of a Church College," *The Christian Scholar* 43 (1960): 25-38.

6. Martin E. Marty, "On Being 'Prophetic,'" *The Christian Century*, 14 May 1980, 559.

7. H. Richard Niebuhr, *Christ and Culture* (New York: Harper & Brothers, 1951).

8. Charles Scriven, *The Transformation of Culture: Christian Social Ethics After H. Richard Niebuhr* (Scottdale, Pa.: Herald Press, 1988), 20.

9. Viktor E. Frankl, *Psychotherapy and Existentialism* (New York: Pocket Books, 1967), 60.

10. Elie Wiesel, *The Forgotten* (New York: Summit Books, 1992), 11-12.

11. T. S. Eliot, *The Complete Poems and Plays: 1909-1950* (New York: Harcourt, Brace & World, Inc., 1971), 96.

12. Bruce Baird-Middleton, dir., *Robert Coles: An Intimate Biographical Interview* [videotape] (Cambridge: Harvard University Press, 1988); *Robert Coles: Teacher* [videotape) (New York: First Run Features, 1991).

13. Donald B. Kraybill, *The Upside-Down Kingdom*, revised ed. (Scottdale, Pa.: Herald Press, 1990).

14. Scriven, 156.

15. Michael Novak, *Ascent of the Mountain, Flight of the Dove: an Invitation to Religious Studies*, revised ed., (New York: Harper & Row), 1978.

PART THREE

Revisions and Outworkings
of the Fresno Pacific College Idea

Chapter 7

The Revision of the Fresno Pacific Collge Idea, 1979-1982: A Contextual and Linguistic Interpretation

Wilfred Martens

Since its inception as Pacific Bible Institute and through its various stages as an institution of the Mennonite Brethren Church, Fresno Pacific College has been shaped by persons who shared a common core of unique values, beliefs, and principles. This core was articulated in the mid-1960s as the "Pacific College Idea." For more than a decade the Idea served the institution and its constituency well. In the late 1970s, however, the college experienced major changes that demanded a review of the core and its embodiment in the Idea.

CONTEXT OF REVISION

In 1979 Edmund Janzen, then president of Fresno Pacific College, initiated a review process of the Idea. Several factors prompted its reappraisal, some internal and others external.

The 1970s were years of significant growth, development and change during the last few years of Arthur Wiebe's presidency (1960-1975) and the first few years of Edmund Janzen's presidency

(1975-1985). A major impetus for growth during the Wiebe era was a federal Title III grant that provided funds for developing institutions. Programs were initiated and promoted: a graduate program in education; an in-service education program that provided workshops, classes, and resources for school districts in the Central Valley area; a Community Lay Training Program, a partnership between FPC, the Mennonite Brethren Biblical Seminary, and churches that offered courses for the "adult lay community." As the college extended its scope geographically and beyond traditional educational boundaries, its constituency became more pluralistic. Through these and other programs the college enlarged and multiplied its essential constituencies.

These programs also required additional faculty and staff. New persons joined the college who were largely unaware of its history and traditions. There were increasing pressures to inform them of foundational matters. Orientation to the Idea was a standard procedure for new persons; however, many were generally unfamiliar and unconnected with its core values. Those in leadership felt the need to connect and reconnect persons to the center to ensure that personnel and programs were integrally related to the whole.

Besides these internal pressures, several external factors precipitated change. In 1979 ownership of the college shifted from the United States Conference of Mennonite Brethren Churches to the Pacific District Conference, a regional entity within the larger national conference. The shift in ownership required a change in college-board-constituency relationships. Prior to the 1979 restructuring, Pacific College was represented on the U.S. Board of Education by six regional representatives. These persons were generally viewed as persons of experience and vision who shared an elevated vision of Christian higher education. After 1979 the board became a regional board with membership elected or appointed from the Pacific District. In those first few years delegates were eager to ensure a level of constituent control. They therefore elected persons to the board who were active and vocal in local congregations but not necessarily experienced in Christian higher education. Some were new to the task of serving as directors of a changing, growing educational institution. Some appeared to have personal agendas: to change a "liberal" college to a more "conservative" one; to shift control from what a few perceived to be a faculty-controlled institution to a board-controlled one; to reshape a provincial denominational college into more conformity with other evangelical Christian colleges such as Westmont, Biola and Wheaton.

Another tension in college-board relationships resulted from a lack of understanding of the board's role by a few inexperienced board members. These persons seemed unfamiliar with the traditional distinction between a board's role of establishing policy and the college administration's role of administering policy. Board chairman Arthur Jost was a positive influence in clarifying the board's role and in cautioning its inexperienced members against interfering in the administration of college affairs.

The year 1979 was also a year of self-study as part of the accreditation review conducted by the Western Association of Schools and Colleges (WASC). The self-study report was presented to the WASC committee in 1980 and accreditation was renewed for an additional five-year period. The WASC committee considered review of the Idea timely and appropriate, and commended the college for its efforts.

In an October 1979 report to the board, President Janzen declared that this was the "year of the church." Behind the declaration was his hope that the new board would "provide a strong vehicle for communication with the churches." He also suggested that "a more church-active faculty is an important goal for the college." These comments were symptomatic of some theological dissonance between college and church constituency. This dissonance had roots that reached back to the PBI years.[1]

A few years later, in October 1993, Edmund Janzen commented on this tension at a faculty workshop. He reflected on his conversations with two persons who were influential in establishing PBI in the mid-1940s and provided leadership in its formative years: Rev. Sam W. Goossen, acting president in 1944, and Rev. Sam Wiens, an instructor in 1944. Both Goossen and Wiens indicated that in promoting PBI as a distinctive Mennonite Brethren institution, they faced some resistance from persons and groups, particularly from the Reedley and Dinuba MB churches, who felt that an MB Bible institute was unnecessary. This resistance came largely from persons who had attended and continued to express strong support for Biola as an institution that had provided, and could continue to provide, appropriate biblical training for MB students. They perceived Biola as an institution with strong emphases on missions, evangelism, personal piety, and biblical study. Janzen further suggested that early opposition to the establishment of PBI was due to the perception that an MB Bible institute might move MB biblical education away from Evangelicalism toward a distinctive MB approach, a move that caused uneasiness among the Biola supporters.[2]

This theological dissonance between Evangelicalism and historical "Mennonitism" or Anabaptism was another factor that created pressure for change in the Idea. A few board members, who claimed to represent popular sentiment in their home churches or areas, wanted to shape Fresno Pacific into greater conformity with some nondenominational Christian colleges, particularly Biola, and therefore considered the Idea, in part or in whole, as inappropriate for an evangelical Christian college sponsored by the Pacific District Conference. It leaned too heavily on historical Anabaptism and obsolete denominational distinctives and not enough on current Evangelicalism.

During the late 1970s the Pacific District Conference was struggling to respond to changes and challenges in district churches. Church leaders were concerned about denominational loyalty. The Board of Reference and Counsel of the PDC commissioned a study paper presented at the 1977 conference by Robert Radke. The paper, "Faithful Church Attendance," stated that "the Mennonite Brethren churches have enjoyed some of the finest and deepest commitments of loyalty to the local church known among evangelicals in the past decades. However, it seems quite apparent that our loyalty and commitment to the local church is in a bad state of affairs."[3]

Loyalty of Mennonite Brethren young people was also a concern of the FPC board. Chairman Arthur Jost reported to the conference in 1980 that "recruitment of Mennonite Brethren students and students in general has been a real concern of the board. . . . It is obvious from the lists of students who are attending our local state colleges and universities that there is a large potential of Mennonite Brethren students who could and should be served at Fresno Pacific College."[4]

Some persons in the Pacific District Conference leadership wanted to see FPC conform more closely to priorities and goals of the conference. William Neufeld, District Minister of the PDC, suggested in 1978 that "Fresno Pacific College needs to continue with a strong emphasis on contemporary ministries, including new church planting as an important emphasis." Then he pointed to another denomination as a model example for training persons in evangelism: "The evangelism . . . program of the First Baptist Church of Modesto is an excellent example."[5]

Thus, the revision of the Idea did not occur on an insulated island of collegiality. Winds and currents of change, both internal and external, helped shape the process and contents of the revised version adopted in 1982.

PROCESS AND CHANGES

In initiating a process of review, President Janzen felt that the faculty needed to be central to the process and therefore recommended a task force of three persons: two regular faculty persons (Delbert Wiens and Wilfred Martens) and the Academic Dean who chaired the committee (Dalton Reimer worked initially with the committee; when he resigned from the dean's position he was replaced by the new dean, Robert Enns, in May 1981). The task force was assigned two general responsibilities: it was to identify the major concerns and issues that needed consideration, and it was to recommend a process by which the entire college community might be involved in the process at appropriate stages.

In an April 1979 memo to the committee, Janzen clarified the task:

The committee (would Goals Committee or Mission and Purpose Committee sound important enough?) has the freedom to consult widely in the community and constituency. . . . The task, as I see it, is to start with a review or analysis of the old "Idea" and redefine, restate, etc., the mission of the College. No doubt the end product will be a mission statement that clearly sets forth the nature and mission of the institution.[6]

On the assumption that the Idea needed revision, the committee spent the first year identifying processes, collecting and studying comparable statements from other colleges (particularly other Mennonite colleges) and reviewing aspects of the existing statement that were in need of change. It was not clear at the early stages whether change was needed in part or in whole.

In early 1981 the committee scheduled several workshops that focused on critical issues related to the Idea. Administrators, board members, faculty, selected pastors, and student leaders participated. A memo outlined the purpose of the workshop:

The appointed task force has suggested that it might be appropriate to invite input from the constituent groups of the college prior to completing a first draft of a revised "Idea" statement. That is the purpose of this workshop. Thus, the intent is not to come to any final conclusions, but rather to explore together how the mission of the college might be articulated in a revised "Idea" statement.[7]

The workshop was designed to focus on two aspects of the college: the concept of "community," and the topic of "graduate, in-service, and adult education." In its original form the Idea was expressed in seven categories:

Pacific College is a Christian College.
Pacific College is a Community.
Pacific College is a Liberal Arts College.
Pacific College is an Experimental College.
Pacific College is an Anabaptist-Mennonite College.
Pacific College is a Non-Sectarian College.
Pacific College is a Prophetic College.

As a result of the workshop, four categories were identified as topics which required clarification, redefinition, and reconsideration:

1. *Fresno Pacific College is a Christian College.* A major concern focused on theological identification, whether the college is—or should be understood as—evangelical, Anabaptist or Christian. Another concern expressed the need for clarity regarding the meaning of "Christian." Some suggested that an important part of the mission of a Christian college was to convert non-Christian students to the faith. Others resisted this interpretation. Among the questions posed for discussion were the following: Are we a missionary community that reaches out to nonbelievers? To whom are we accountable regarding theology, educational philosophy, and lifestyle matters? The latter question was directed to those who leaned toward a nondenominational stance.

2. *Fresno Pacific College is a Liberal Arts College.* Two concerns were raised in response to this statement. One focused on the need for clearer definition regarding the appropriateness of career training and professional programs in a liberal arts college. Another called for more clarity regarding relationships with other institutions such as Mennonite Brethren Biblical Seminary and California State University, Fresno. The college was experimenting with concurrent enrollment arrangements with these and other institutions.

3. *Fresno Pacific College is a Community.* The term "community," a word with several connotations, prompted a wide range of responses. One such response by Robert Enns, Professor of Sociology, listed six reasons in support of revising the existing statement. His response was an example of the many questions and concerns raised about this category:

1. The language of the statement is sexist. . . .
2. The statement is individualistic. . . .

3. The statement speaks too narrowly to the education of persons at one stage in the human life cycle. . . .
4. The statement is static. . . .
5. The statement does not recognize the plurality of communities in which we are all embedded and which we serve. . . .
6. We receive the support or a variety or communities and structures. . . . The statement might attempt to make more clear that there are mutual responsibilities inherent in these multiple relationships.[8]

4. Fresno Pacific College is a Church-Related College. The mission of the college was suggested in the form of a biblical analogy that illustrates two forms of leadership: priest and prophet. Two questions expressed the ambiguity of the role of a denominationally-sponsored college. First, how do we define our priestly role? That is, how do we affirm, support, and assist the Mennonite Brethren Church? Second, how do we define our prophetic role? That is, how do we serve as an institution of leadership? How do we encourage change?

A second workshop in March coincided with the college board meeting and therefore made possible faculty and board participation. Three topics were selected as the focus of the workshop: "Anabaptist Christian, or just Christian?," "Professional and Liberal Arts Education," and "Church and College Relationships."

As a result of the workshops, and after receiving feedback from groups and individuals, members of the review committee, in November 1981, began to formulate a draft of a revised Idea statement. They agreed on two principles: retaining the original form but infusing it with current concerns, and reducing the original seven categories to four. Three categories would be retained: "FPC is a Christian College," "FPC is a Community," and "FPC is a Liberal Arts College."

Three of the original categories were to be subsumed as part of the three listed above and not identified therefore as distinct categories: "FPC is an Experimental College," "FPC is an Anabaptist-Mennonite College," and "FPC is a Non-Sectarian College." Some considered the original section on FPC as an "Experimental College" to be inappropriate. To some, it implied that the college was a research institution, although FPC has not emphasized research as a major academic discipline. Others responded positively, suggesting that to be an experimental college was important, but that it not be highlighted as a distinct category. They preferred that it be an inherent part of the whole Idea statement. A few expressed fear that the college might be perceived as "experimenting" with its theology and biblical foundations if this aspect received too much prominence.

Regarding the category "FPC is a Non-Sectarian College," there was little controversy. It was generally agreed that it could be subsumed in other categories or integrated into the document as a whole. Hence, it was deleted as a distinctive section.

The section dealing with FPC as an "Anabaptist-Mennonite College" received considerable attention and was cause for intensive debate. Some who objected to the term "Anabaptist" preferred to have the college aligned more with evangelical colleges such as Westmont, Biola, and Azusa Pacific. The term "Anabaptist" had uncomfortable connotations for others who defined it narrowly in reference to pacifism, community, and other aspects associated with the counter-culture movement of the 1960s.

In 1979 the PDC Board of Reference and Counsel commissioned a study paper on pacifism. Entitled, "The Practical Application of Love and Nonresistance," it was written and presented by Edmund Janzen. According to Janzen, the problem "focuses on the serious reservations that some pastors, members, and churches have concerning its inclusion in the *Confession of Faith*." Such persons feel that "nonresistance is an optional distinctive of earlier Anabaptism that really is not a viable teaching for our time." In citing reasons for the problem he suggests that persons opposed to nonresistance feel that "the nonresistance stance has been co-opted by those who are not motivated by the teachings of Christ—the radical left, humanists, revolutionaries, counter culture proponents who espouse the view to achieve their own ends. They are viewed negatively by society." In citing another reason he stated that opponents may feel that "The nonresistance stance has been politicized. To be nonresistant is to be an enemy of the State. The marriage of Christian faith to American politics has bred a civil religion that brands nonresistance as un-American and unpatriotic."[9] Largely as the result of such differences within the PDC, the faculty agreed to a revised version in which the word was eliminated and the ideas of peace and nonresistance were expressed in a more subdued manner.

The category "FPC is a Prophetic College" also received considerable discussion. In workshops that included pastors and parishioners, faculty, staff, administrators and board members, there were various perspectives on the meaning and role of the Christian liberal arts college.

President Janzen in a workshop presentation reviewed some sources of misunderstanding and tension between church and college. The church expects the college to teach, to train, and to lead, yet if it moves beyond constituency expectations, it is considered subversive. The church expects the college to practice critical thinking and to raise and examine issues, yet the constituency becomes uncomfortable when these are applied to the church. He called for the college to be both priest and prophet. As priest it trains and prepares students for a role in the church. It reminds students of denominational history and distinctives, and encourages them to grow in the faith. As prophet it calls for accountability of biblical principles. It clarifies distinctions between culture and Kingdom, and deals with moral and ethical issues of culture and society. As both priest and prophet, the college serves a pastoral role as well as a leadership role.

To improve communication and relationships between college and churches, President Janzen in 1979 created the Church Advisory Council (CAC). Its primary purpose was to serve as liaison between the district conference and the college. The CAC, which met twice a year, served as a source of communication, feedback, and counsel. Although it was generally agreed that the CAC served to bring churches and the college into closer relationships, not all its actions were deemed appropriate. For example, in its 1980 report to the conference, the CAC said it would make available to church members a "Gripe-A-Gram." Born out of a populist slogan—"Remember, we want to hear what people are thinking . . . then resolve the concern"—it carried the unfortunate suggestion that the CAC was interested only in soliciting negative comments. In fact it was interested in much more.[10]

It was important to board members and administrators that the revised Idea have the support of the church, college, and constituency. Arthur Jost, chairman of the board, supported a comprehensive approach to and broad participation in the revision process. In a letter to the board on October 10, 1981, he stated, "I further appeal to the Board to assist the school in updating the 'Fresno Pacific College Idea.' Some additional work needs to be done. . . . The Board must, in the next several months, formulate policies so that the new directions of the college can be monitored."[11] Three board members were appointed to work with the review committee: Jim Holm, a graduate of the college and then pastor of a large congregation in Lodi, California; Peter J. Klassen, a former faculty member and then an administrator at California State University, Fresno; and Harold Enns, also a former FPC faculty member and then a businessman and leader in the Reedley Mennonite Brethren congregation.

On December 10, 1981, the review committee presented two drafts — a short and long version — of the revised Idea to a faculty workshop. The brief version was intended for "external" or "public" purposes; the longer version for "internal" college purposes. Both versions included three sections:

FPC is a Christian College
FPC is a Liberal Arts College
FPC is Community

In responding to the drafts, several faculty members expressed concern that the idea of the college as experimental was too subdued in the revised version, and that the Anabaptist emphasis and distinctives of the earlier version was too weak. As a result the revision resulted in a lack of clarity regarding purpose. Did it reflect reality (who we are), or the ideal (who we can be)? At the conclusion of the workshop the faculty affirmed the work of the review committee and encouraged it to proceed with the longer version. The shorter version was considered superficial and inadequate.

From December 1981 until the fall of 1982 the Review Committee worked with persons and small groups representing the board, administration and faculty. There continued to be general agreement regarding the three categories and the general content. The committee spent considerable time with words, phrases and editorial matters that changed the draft from its December 1981 version.

Changes tended to revolve around four topics, each of which represented tensions between the college and its MB constituency, between a segment of faculty (those who wished to ensure a strong Anabaptist-Mennonite identity, in particular) and a segment of the board (those who desired a less "provincial" Mennonite tone and a more "evangelical" content), and within the faculty and board (there was not a clear consensus within either):

1. The term "Anabaptist" continued to cause discomfort. Those who opposed its inclusion thought that it identified the college too closely with a sect that was perceived to practice communal life, unpatriotic pacifism, and a rejection of societal values, practices and traditions.

2. Terms such as "peace," "peacemakers" and "justice" were debated for reasons similar to those associated with "Anabaptism."

3. The term "community" had connotations that were perceived in various ways. Opponents associated it with the communal movements of the 1960s and expressed the desire for a less "loaded" term.

4. Although it was generally conceded that terms associated with the "priestly" and "prophetic" roles of the college might be included, there was not a clear consensus on whether these should receive equal emphasis or whether the former should be more prominent than the latter.

By the fall of 1982 the administration was anxious to move the document toward adoption. The Review Committee (Robert Enns, Wilfred Martens, Delbert Wiens and Paul Toews) tended to lean toward identifying the college as a distinctive Anabaptist institution. The committee, however, worked hard to provide alternatives, to compromise and to restate concepts and expression so that the revision might move forward toward adoption.

One of the final tasks of the Review Committee was to assign Wilfred Martens, Professor of English, to write an introduction to the document, which subsequently gave focus to the three sections. In a parallel structure, the introduction included three aspects:

1. "The Fresno Pacific Idea is a guide for the future; it is also a process of the present and an outgrowth of the past."

The first clause suggested that a primary purpose of the revised Idea was to serve as an ideal, a vision that was not yet realized. It was not to be merely a reflection of the present status of the college. The second clause suggested that the Idea was dynamic, and that the college and church were to be engaged in a process of interpreting, discerning, and understanding it. The third clause suggested that the revised version was rooted historically in a cultural and biblical tradition, in an educational journey that included the stories of persons, families, groups, churches, and faculties.

2. "As the college seeks to discern the future, understand the present, and interpret the past, it affirms the significance of knowledge which leads to wisdom, encourages virtue, establishes harmony, and creates balance and perspective."

The second paragraph brought together Greek and Hebrew ideals: knowledge and the community of values. It affirmed the centrality of knowledge in Christian higher education, but did so within the context of the values of Jesus and the Kingdom.

3. "As a Christian liberal arts college, Fresno Pacific College is an integral part of the mission of the church. Through the liberal arts, the college provides knowledge and experience which lead toward

a more perceptive and creative relationship with God, humanity, and the world. The college is a community in which interpersonal relationships play a vital role in the process of education."

The primary purpose of the third paragraph was to introduce the three categories that follow in the revised statement. It affirmed the relationship between church and college. It suggested a unique approach to the liberal arts and to vocational education. And it declared the importance of community as an integral part of education.

The Review Committee recommended to the October 1982 sessions of the board "that the document be adopted to serve as the mission statement of the college with the option for review, perhaps annually."[12] The board overwhelmingly adopted the recommendation.

REFLECTIONS

The second half of the 1970s was a time of major change for the college. Sometimes the college was forced to react and respond; at other times it stretched and reached ahead. The supporting denomination was also experiencing change, clarifying its own mission and looking ahead to the future.

During this period the Mennonite Brethren Conference engaged in a process of redefining the role of its colleges. For Tabor College and FPC these were times of ambiguity and uncertainty, but also times of creativity and opportunity. The MB Church also was experiencing change. Some church members and groups in the late 1970s were still reacting to the 1960s, to the cultural phenomenon of hippies, peace activists, marches and demonstrations, drugs, Vietnam, and communal movements. These persons wanted their church-related college to remain aloof from that image of the 1960s. Others, influenced by church-growth movements, considered some aspects of Anabaptism to be detrimental to church growth and development. These persons and groups encouraged the college to divest itself of historical baggage and controversial theological issues connoted by terms such as peace, nonresistance, prophetic community, liberal arts, and cultural critique.

The period of the late 1970s and early 1980s was a difficult time for colleges and universities, private and public alike. Institutions competed for limited resources. Competition for students was intense. As a result, there was also pressure from a few on the board and in the constituency to reconsider the denominational stance of the college. These persons considered Christian colleges such as Biola, Westmont, and Wheaton to be more appropriate models, with potential for growth, more students, a broader constituency, and increased financial support.

The appointment of Edmund Janzen as president in 1975 with a mandate from the board to improve relationships between church and college seemed propitious. When corporate responsibility for the college shifted from the United States Conference to the Pacific District Conference, the latter did not completely understand the "child" that it had adopted: the child already had a thirty-five-year history; it was growing, maturing, developing, changing.

During those thirty-five years, a nucleus of faculty and administrators, supported by a few visionary board members and constituents, shaped an institution known for its creative approach to education, a college that emphasized the integration of faith and scholarship, a school built on Anabaptist principles that rested on a biblical foundation and on the lessons of the Kingdom. Through the storm and stress of these years, church and college survived and increasingly enjoyed a closer relationship. With such an environment of change, it is not surprising that the Idea served as a lightning rod in the turbulence of the times.

NOTES

1. Annual Report of Fresno Pacific College to the Board of Directors, 20 October 1979, Fresno Pacific College Board of Directors Records, Center for Mennonite Brethren Studies, Fresno, Calif. [Hereafter CMBS].

2. Comment delivered by Edmund Janzen at the Fresno Pacific College Fall Faculty Workshop, 22 October 1993.

3. Robert Radke, "Faithful Church Attendance," in *Yearbook of the Sixty-eighth Pacific District Conference of Mennonite Brethren, Blaine, Washington, November 11, 12, 13, 1977,* 44. [All Yearbooks cited hereafter as PDC Yearbook].

4. Arthur Jost, "Fresno Pacific College Report," in 1980 PDC Yearbook, 11.

5. William Neufeld, "Report of the District Minister," 1978 PDC Yearbook, 5.

6. Edmund Janzen to members of the Idea Review Committee, 4 April 1979, Fresno Pacific College Idea Review Committee Records, CMBS.

7. This memo appeared as part of the schedule for a workshop on the FPC Idea Review, held at the Airport Holiday Inn on 25 February 1981, Fresno Pacific College Idea Review Committee Records, CMBS.

8. Robert Enns to members of FPC Idea Review Committee, 29 August 1980, Fresno Pacific Idea Review Committee Records, CMBS.

9. Edmund Janzen, "The Practical Application of Love and Nonresistance," 1979 PDC Yearbook, 45.

10. Kelly Suess, "Advisory Council Report," 1980 PDC Yearbook, 16.

11. Arthur Jost to members of the Board of Directors, 9 October 1981. Attachment to Minutes: Fresno Pacific College Board of Directors, 10 October 1981, Fresno Pacific College Board of Directors Records, CMBS.

12. Minutes: Fresno Pacific College Board of Directors, 30 October 1982, Fresno Pacific College Board of Directors Records, CMBS.

Chapter 8

From Monastery to Marketplace: Idea and Mission in Graduate and Professional Programs at Fresno Pacific College

John Yoder

At fifty years of age, Fresno Pacific College is heir to a rich story of people, events and ideas woven into a complex and multifaceted tapestry. An important part of the story has centered on the college's struggle to define its identity and mission within the larger context of Anabaptist/Mennonite thought and American Christian higher education.

The college's understanding of its mission and self-identity has developed through various forms over the years, but there have been at least three major strands clearly identifiable in the broader weaving. The first of these can be found in the initial vision of the founders of what was to become the Pacific Bible Institute. Among those with this early vision there was a strong sense of the need to prepare Christians who would lead and serve in the Mennonite Brethren Church. Their vision included Bible training and preparation for those who might enter the pastorate but also offered preparation for workers in many other kinds of church work such as Christian education, youth work, and home and foreign missions.[1] The essence of this vision lay in the school's commitment to "preparation for service." This initial vision was perhaps not so different in kind from those that followed as it was different in its emphasis on immediate application of the training being offered. The use of the word "training" in the early catalogs to refer to its programs contrasts with the later use of "education" as the college moved toward a liberal arts curriculum.

In its simplest form the second strand of self-understanding has been woven around the development and interpretation of the "Fresno Pacific Idea." The Idea in its various forms has provided a philosophical and theological center from which the college sought to develop an understanding of its fundamental purpose and its self-concept. The self understanding arising from this process has drawn on the tradition of European higher education, as re-invented by the American post-revolutionary colleges. It also has drawn on a yet older tradition in which the university is an agent for transmitting moral values and particular religious traditions.[2] In contrast to the first, more practical and applied self-understanding, the focus now shifted to an "educative" mode in which direct application of the curriculum was of secondary concern.

Here the focus shifted to a more or less classical undergraduate curriculum within the context of a Christian community committed to an Anabaptist view of the church and the world as a paradigm through which to interpret the liberal arts. Among other things, this paradigm embodied a vision of mission in which to be "significant" was to carry out a prophetic role in the Mennonite Brethren Church, American higher education, and in the world at large.[3] It was a vision that sought to bring together the best of the traditional liberal arts and Anabaptist/Mennonite thought into a unified center that would serve as the college's *raison d'etre*. Not all members of the community shared the same depth of understanding and commitment to that vision but its influence has been pervasive and has fundamentally shaped the college as it exists today.

Beginning in the mid-to-late 1960s, a third strand of self-understanding developed in the tapestry that is Fresno Pacific's story. It was a strand that ran counter to the one centered directly on the Idea. In some ways it had more in common with the earlier service orientation of the Bible institute days, though the focus was not so much on service to the church as to society. It was also a strand in which the notions of mission and philosophy were more implicit than explicit. This was a more pragmatic, less ideological vision that took its cues for mission from the needs of the surrounding educational community and sought to define a more contemporary and immediate notion of the college's purpose. Broadly, this was to "do good" by responding to immediate needs perceived within the public education community.

This more pragmatic mission was expressed in the development of pre-service, in-service and professional development programs for educators in the elementary and high schools of Fresno County and the surrounding area. Graduate programs leading to a Master of Arts in Education would follow later. Though the college had begun offering courses leading to a teacher credential earlier, the increased emphasis on professional and vocational programs was problematic to faculty committed to the more pure vision of the liberal arts. Many of the liberal arts faculty found the new professional programs to be entrepreneurial, non-ideological, lacking academic integrity and distant from the original core foci of the college.

Though not usually explicit, this more pragmatic vision was also driven by the need of the college to reach a higher level of financial stability. The revenue from the professional programs provided genuine relief for the hard-pressed college budget. To some it was an open question whether the college could have survived during those lean years without the revenue generated by the professional programs.[4] The "practitioners" in the faculty found it ironic that while the professional programs helped to ensure the college's survival, at least some "liberal arts purists" in the faculty continued to interpret the more professional enterprises as selling out the institution's soul for the sake of expediency.[5] The practitioners who were developing professional programs in education had trouble understanding how their colleagues could miss the point that in the "real world" you also had to find ways to pay the bills.[6]

Motivations are, of course, rarely pure and are often complex. To the professional educators [i.e., the practitioners] in the faculty there was much more to the story than simple entrepreneurial zeal. For them, the growth of the education programs was a response to deeply felt concerns about the needs of an increasingly beleaguered public educational establishment, that was in turn trying to meet the needs of an increasingly dysfunctional society. The vision for these programs grew out of their belief that bringing a Christian ethic and world view into the professional arena was an appropriate expression of Christian concern. Such a conviction grew out of the belief that one served God by serving local and immediate needs. Helping educators become better informed, more competent, more caring, more dedicated, more loving professionals was, in their view, a concrete and legitimate expression of the servant-leadership ideals expressed in the Idea. While the purists were suspicious of this reasoning as after-the-fact rationalization, the practitioners argued that these opportunities offered the potential for a happy marriage between a concrete expression of mission and institutional survival.

To understand the intensity of the ongoing debate about the college mission, one must recognize that for those attempting to define and shape Fresno Pacific College during the 1960s and 1970s, the college was not simply an institution. It was an idea, an ideal, an experiment in Mennonite, Anabaptist and Christian higher education. The college was to be a kind of testing ground for the possibility of merging Anabaptist/Mennonite thought with academic respectability.[7] It was to be a forum within which an alternative to the corruption of the surrounding academic and even churchly culture could be articulated. The college would do so by defining and embodying a radical option that took a different point of departure in shaping its understanding of the world and that looked to a distinctive set of ideas as a definitional core. That core was articulated in the Fresno Pacific College Idea. Though the Idea would go through several critical revisions, it has remained centered on the essential components that have come to define the college's fundamental commitments: to be Christian and Anabaptist, to be centered on the liberal arts, to practice community, and to be in some way both experimental and prophetic.

PERSONAL AND IDEOLOGICAL THREADS

The genesis of a Mennonite Brethren institution of higher education on the West Coast lay in the perceived need for Bible-centered education and training for young people who would provide service and leadership to the church and would engage in mission to the "world." The central rationale was clear: to train young people for "the work of pastors, evangelists, Sunday School workers, missionaries and personal soul winners."[8] The expansion of the original vision to include a broader liberal arts curriculum came fifteen years later because of an increased awareness of the limitations of a Bible institute curriculum.[9] Shifting the curricular focus to the liberal arts meant, among other things, a de-emphasis on development of "skills for ministry," focusing instead on concern about knowing and understanding the world from a Christian point of view. It was a shift from focusing on "doing" toward a focus on "being."

It was still later, in 1965, that the college Board of Directors approved a proposal for developing a professional program to educate teachers,[10] followed a few years later by graduate level courses in education. Again there was at least an implicit re-orientation of the college's mission and identity. In one sense this change was a shift back toward a focus on education for application but this time at the professional, instead of churchly, level. It is also true that this change is probably more correctly characterized as an "expansion" of mission and identity rather than a "shift" since the new program did not replace existing ones but represented instead a widening of focus. In any case, the new programs brought with them some sense of disequilibrium and generated debate within the faculty as to the appropriateness of their fit within the college mission and identity as it was then understood.

It was arguably, however, Arthur Wiebe's arrival as president of the college in 1960 that set the stage for these developments. As a former high school science teacher and principal, author of a widely used secondary school science text and member of a major science education project at Stanford University, Wiebe's interest in secondary education was self-evident.

Three years after his arrival as President, Arthur Wiebe brought Elias Wiebe onto the faculty as Dean. He too came with a strong background of experience and interest in education, especially at the elementary level. When the State of California mandated fifth-year, post-baccalaureate preparation for elementary and high school teachers, it was only natural to the "educators" that this was an opportunity toward which the college should move. In 1967 Arthur Wiebe recommended to the faculty that Elias Wiebe be asked to develop a teacher education program that draws upon the "most imaginative and effective teacher education program[s] [in the country]."[11]

Some five years after the development of the Teacher Education program, Silas Bartsch, a former high school teacher, principal and district superintendent, joined the teacher education faculty with a special interest in developing programs to provide in-service or professional development training programs for practicing teachers. Like both Arthur and Elias Wiebe, Bartsch brought with him an intense interest in elementary and secondary education and a keen awareness of its needs. During his tenure in the schools and as a district superintendent Bartsch experienced firsthand the need for quality in-service programs for teachers. He pursued a vision for developing a multifaceted program to address those needs.

By combining the interests of persons such as Arthur Wiebe, Elias Wiebe and Silas Bartsch, it was probably predictable that there would be an expansion of the education programs at the college. Among other things, they established what was at first called the "Department of Extension Education." This program included non-credit professional education courses that typically were offered on the school sites and were geared to the needs of practicing teachers. A few years later that department became the department of In-service and Off-campus Programs and still later was renamed as the "Division of Professional Development," with a mission to provide professional education courses for educators in the elementary and secondary schools. Meanwhile, federal grants for programs in the teaching of reading and later in mathematics generated additional momentum for expanded in-service efforts in those areas. In 1974 the college approved planning for programs leading to a Masters of Arts in Education. Accreditation for the Master of Arts was formalized in 1975. As with earlier developments in education programs, development of the Master of Arts program in Education was a logical extension of an already established direction.

In 1975, Arthur Wiebe left the college presidency to devote more time to the graduate program in math and science education. Wiebe later went on to found and direct the AIMS Foundation, a highly successful, not-for-profit organization devoted to development of curricular materials and training teachers for the integration of math and science.

But Arthur Wiebe was not only interested in the education of teachers. He was also a college administrator and scholar aware of contemporary thinking in American higher education as well as the growing body of "renewal scholarship" in the Anabaptist tradition. Alongside his interests and efforts in developing programs in education, Wiebe set out to find young scholars for his faculty that would place the college on the cutting edge of American higher education and of Anabaptist/Mennonite scholarship. The resulting mixture of ideologies became the seedbed for the intellectual and ideological ferment that have since characterized Fresno Pacific College.[12]

Was the development of professional programs at Pacific, then, the result of a deliberate outworking of the Idea, or was it primarily a pragmatic, even opportunistic, response to circumstances? There is evidence that both the Board of Directors and the Administration struggled with this question and the tension that it generated. Nor was it clear to all that these were necessarily antithetical. Joel Wiebe cites a June 1970 document that refers to "Elias Wiebe and Silas Bartsch's [proposal for a] pioneer program of in-service training that promises to become a major service and public relations device"[13] (otherwise understood to mean: "a major fund raising and recruiting tool")[14] with no reference to the core ideological vision and purposes. Simultaneously, partly because of pressure from the liberal arts faculty, there was an ongoing struggle to bring such efforts into harmony with the fundamental college mission and the ideology expressed in the Idea. A proposal in the early 1970s for establishing a "Master of Arts in Teaching," for example, was concerned that a "Christian view of life and knowledge" be at the "core" of that proposed program.[15]

The 1977 proposal for a Masters degree program in Administrative Services took this notion a step further with references to "current social problems" as a rationale for that program's development. This proposal noted further the expectations expressed in the "Institutional Policy for Professional Preparation Programs," that in order to be consistent with the "basic objectives of the institution" students in professional programs must "always be required to have a significant concentration in the liberal arts tradition" and further that, as both "experimental" and "prophetic," the college was broadly concerned that it serve as a "center of independent critique of all man's endeavors" and should function as a "conscience of society and the Church."[16] The 1984 minutes of the Graduate Council reflect the continuing struggle: seeking to articulate what was taking place programmatically with the college's core ideology, and to bring the "secular" aspects of the "philosophy statement discussion" into correlation with the "values and commitment" aspects.[17]

These statements notwithstanding, it is difficult to identify concrete expressions of those sentiments in the curricular and programmatic designs being developed during this time. The absence of curricular expressions of the philosophical statements suggests that the primary vehicle for implementing the philosophical statements of the professional programs was to be found in the professional conduct and the witness of the lives of those administering and teaching in the programs. This notion was made explicit in the minutes of the Graduate Council, which stress the importance of "modeling" by the teacher: "It is who we are that matters."[18] Given this stance it is ironic that much of the hands-on instruction was being carried out by adjunct faculty who were hired from the public sector by program directors and who were not subject to review or affirmation by the faculty or the institution.

Nevertheless, the "Graduate Program Mission Statement," which was approved by the Board of Trustees in 1985, seems to have been a further reflection of this struggle to respond to questions about the purpose and legitimacy of the education programs and was, in the end, far more than just a statement of mission or objectives. This statement sought to articulate a broader theological and philosophical basis for doing professional education (at the graduate level, in this case). It also sought to place the work of the graduate division into the mainstream of the college's larger mission and focus. The statement was divided into three sections focusing respectively on the Vision, Identity and Leadership of the Graduate Program. In each section there was a series of philosophical and theological beliefs followed by statements of commitment.

The 1985 statement sought to place the mission of the graduate, professional division within the overall mission of the college and the church as well as within a framework of a "clearly Evangelical-Mennonite . . . orientation, with its emphasis on discipleship, commitment and Christian community informing a unified Christian view of life and knowledge." The "vision" of the program was interpreted, among other things, as focusing on "character formation in the image of God . . . preparing [students] for vocation and service" and called for the "integration of faith and learning, of the liberal arts and career development." In its efforts to bring together the applied, professional orientation of the graduate programs with the liberal arts curriculum, the statement took a broad view of the purposes of the liberal arts. Simultaneously it implied a philosophical commitment to a kind of "witness of presence" and of modeling in contrast to the more overtly Christian content of the undergraduate curriculum.

It is not clear from the statement whether it was primarily intended to be descriptive or prescriptive. That is, whether it was to define what was thought to already exist or to serve as an ideal toward which the division should strive. In any case, the statement called for committed Christian leadership to provide an "alternative" and "innovative" program that would take its identity from the larger college and from its relation to the church and that further sought to bring a Christian perspective and presence to the professional arena of education.

Whether adopting this statement of mission increased the acceptability of the education programs to the larger college is unclear. What does seem clear is that the professional programs were never really able to find concrete expressions for some of their more ambitious goals such as shaping a programmatic identity out of the college's relation to the church. Nevertheless, the statement seems significant in several ways. First, it attempted to place the graduate programs clearly within the mainstream of the college, though it suggested that the undergraduate program should remain clearly at the "center." The statement also implicitly proposed that it was possible to "do" professional education within the context of a Christian/Mennonite liberal arts college without violating the central tenets of the institutional mission. The statement was built upon the implicit proposition that the Kingdom of God can be carried forward by a program that moves persons or institutions in some way closer to the realities of the "Kingdom ethics" of love and concern for individuals, and that such programs are, in their own right, legitimate expressions of the college's broader ministry.

A few years later, in 1988, the department of In-service and Off-campus Programs developed its own purpose and mission statement including a statement on "Education as Mission" drafted by Howard Loewen, a member of the Board of Trustees and a professor of theology at the Mennonite Brethren Biblical Seminary.[19] The statement carried further the attempt to position the professional education programs as an outworking of the central college mission, casting them "as a direct extension of the educational mission of [the college]."[20]

In 1991 the graduate division again undertook a review of the graduate mission statement. The intent was to develop a more focused statement that would clarify the purposes of the division while maintaining the centrality of the tenets contained in the Idea. Though much shorter than the 1985 version, the resulting statement, formally adopted by the Board of Trustees in 1992, did not differ significantly from the 1985 statement in direction or orientation. The revised statement continued to position the graduate programs within the college's historical and ideological framework. Like the previous one, the 1992 statement referred to the foundational basis of the liberal arts, the college's historical distinctives, the importance of community and of providing servant-leadership to the church and the academic/professional community.

The 1992 graduate mission statement did, however, make two substantive departures from the 1985 version. First, the graduate program and mission were defined without reference to the undergraduate program, though retaining the notion of the liberal arts as foundational. This legitimated, in effect, the graduate program as an academic division of the college in its own right. Second, the mission statement deliberately used language that did not restrict graduate programs to those in education, thus opening the door to possible development of graduate and professional programs in other areas.

Taken together, these aspects of the new mission statement suggested a new level of maturity for the graduate division and the possibility of an expanded notion of mission for the division and for the college.

The paradox that comes from juxtaposing idealism against pragmatism is often troublesome, and thus it is hardly surprising that Fresno Pacific was not able to resolve that tension, even as an abstraction. But the faculty, operating from the more pragmatic paradigm, struggled to shake off the perception that there was, indeed, an element of retro-activity in their work on integration of ideology and mission: a kind of after-the-fact justification for the expediency of developing professionally oriented programs.[21]

Fresno Pacific's struggle to bring together the liberal arts and the professions was not unique. This inherent tension has been reflected with varying degrees of intensity in the larger historical stream of American higher education since the last quarter of the nineteenth century. The experience of Fresno Pacific is to some extent a replication of this older struggle. The expansion of manufacturing and commercial agriculture during the latter part of the nineteenth century, along with major influxes of new immigrants into the country, produced demands for a "new kind of graduate" from American colleges and universities.[22] Such a graduate needed to be more closely attuned to the needs of the business and professional world. The faculties in those institutions too, "resisted changes that might corrupt the classical foundations of the college curriculum and undermine the close-knit communities of scholars created in the image of Thomas Jefferson's academical village."[23]

The land-grant colleges west of the Mississippi River were a further response to the pressure for a "new kind of college." They attempted to unite the classical curriculum of the post-colonial colleges with a more applied, vocationally-oriented curriculum. That goal, however, raised questions within the institutions about how they were to maintain integrity and coherence and about how such a diverse faculty could share values and maintain collegiality. Historian Clara Lovett argues that the issue of the coherence of the higher education curriculum remains unresolved to the present day even "after a century of debates, culture wars, reforms and counter-reforms."[24] That Fresno Pacific College is caught up in these debates suggests that the college had found its way into one of the fundamental debates in mainstream American higher education.

From Idea to Mission

From the 1960s to the present, the Fresno Pacific Idea, in its various permutations, has served to focus the faculty's concern with ideology. The faculty (and the board) labored long and hard to express their understanding of what it meant to be a Mennonite, Christian, liberal arts college.

The resulting Idea statement was an attempt to articulate something of that understanding. It was also a product of its age. As indicated earlier, the Idea's roots can be found in the classical notions of the liberal arts. They can also be found in both the intellectual ferment in American higher education of the 1960s and in the in the mid-twentieth-century Mennonite "recovery of the Anabaptist vision." The Idea served as an expression of an ideal in both areas. It was an attempt to stake out a territory that would define the college within the best traditions of scholarship in American higher education and within the renewed scholarly interest in Anabaptism.

In its earlier versions, the Idea contained five essential elements: the college as a Christian institution, as a liberal arts institution, as a community, as experimental and as prophetic. Strictly interpreted, such a statement left little room for developing professional programs. Delbert Wiens noted, for example, that the "liberating arts" are not intended for those who would engage in the "servile" tasks of "hewing wood and drawing water." "Genuinely higher education," he maintained, did not have "getting a job" as its goal.[25]

So how does an institution get from the abstract principles of the Idea to programmatic mission in a professional arena? Is it possible to make a connection and, if so, what does the Idea have to offer to professional education or vice versa? Before exploring this question, a brief summary is needed of the Idea's essence.

In its present form, the Idea consists of three essential components: the notion of a college that is Christian; that is centered upon the liberal arts; and that is committed to community. It is possible to extrapolate theological, educational and professional statements from these essential elements of the Idea. Though obviously not complete by itself, such extrapolation could be construed to make a statement about the nature of God and of his Kingdom, to offer a point of departure for a philosophy of education and an approach to understanding teaching and learning, and to provide some clues about how one might understand professionalism. The Mission Statement of the Graduate Division, as revised and adopted in 1992, was intended to serve as this kind of intermediary link between the Fresno Pacific College Idea and its expression in graduate level, professional programs.

The Graduate Mission Statement begins with the assertion that the central purpose of all divisional activity is to "build and to extend the Kingdom of God." Building upon the Idea's premise of the college as fundamentally Christian, the statement implies that, somehow, "building the Kingdom of God," serves as a touchstone and as a criterion for making decisions about programs and about program objectives within the division.

The statement identifies four particular aspects of this more general mandate. The first defines the philosophical and theological foundation for graduate (and professional) education; next is a broad statement of vision, followed in turn by two statements concerned with ways of doing education and of carrying out a professional role. The implied progression within the statement that begins with a foundational premise, moves to a statement of vision and then to concluding statements applicable to the professional arena is intentional. It serves as a bridge between the abstractions of the idea and the concreteness of the professions.

The first derivation of the general principle of "kingdom building" is a broad foundational statement reflecting the theological and philosophical premises for the division's programs and curricula: "foundational [values] . . . include the essential unity of knowledge under God; the Lordship of Christ over all of life and the integration of faith and learning." While laying out the philosophical underpinnings of the graduate curricula this statement does not, other than in the most global terms, suggest specific programmatic foci or curricular content. Its intention is to provide both a rationale and a platform from which to envision program and curriculum.

This statement is followed by a statement of the vision toward which divisional goals are ultimately directed. This vision includes "[an integrative view of the] liberal arts [as a way of] encouraging reflection on personal, institutional and societal values [as a basis for developing] a vision for personal and societal change . . . which unites theory and practice." It includes further a "commitment to peace, justice and reconciliation as the basis for all relationships . . . recognizing justice as the basis for peace, reconciliation as the goal in resolving conflicts and love as the foundation of all relationships."

Among other things, then, the vision represents both a way of perceiving the world and a commitment to a particular ethic that seeks to embody the principles of God's kingdom. It is vision centered on a set of values and a system of morality from which to critique the prevailing culture and by which to offer an alternative vision of social order based on reconciliation, peace and justice. There is also an embedded commitment to a prophetic function in the division's programs: to point to a better way and to be agents for change.

Third, the statement offers a view of community that has implications for both how one understands teaching and learning and how one might facilitate those processes: "[The relationship between] teachers and learners are . . . characterized by mutual respect, trust, collaboration, [and] shared decision-making. . . . Teaching and learning are understood [as] a common search for truth and wholeness."

The statement broadens the context for community in this section, asserting that

> Diversity is believed to enrich community . . . [and] . . . ethnic and religious identity [are] affirmed as a basis for respectful pluralism. . . . International and ecological relationships . . . provide . . . [a] basis for . . . global consciousness which transcends the . . . limits of nationalism, individualism and isolationism.

The notion of learning in community, then, implies a collaborative view of the learning process and stands in stark contrast to the pervasive individualism of both academic and popular contemporary culture. Learning as an exercise that takes place in community provides the basis for an interactive, constructionist pedagogy. It implies a process in which teacher and student engage in a mutual process of discovery and understanding and in which meaning is constructed by all who participate in the interaction.

Finally, the statement positions both the faculty and the institution in the role of the "servant leader": "The faculty and the programs seek to model both servanthood and leadership. Programs are developed . . . as expressions of the college's leadership role in offering such service."

To lead, in this sense, is also to be "prophetic." It is to offer a critique of prevailing professional values and practice; to offer an alternative way of both being and doing in a professional context based upon a foundational center and an articulated vision. When combined with the previously described view of community, this kind of leadership implies a kind of leading from within. This kind of leadership stands within the world in order to engage it, identifying with those one seeks to serve even as one offers the possibility a change and of a better way.

MONASTERY AND MARKETPLACE

The medieval European monastery and its relationship to the surrounding culture may offer a useful metaphor for reflecting on the Christian college and its relation to the surrounding culture. The metaphor may additionally help to illuminate the juxtaposition and the tension between the liberal arts and the professions at Fresno Pacific College. Christian monasteries were established in medieval Europe as an expression of a particular set of ideas about religious order and service. They were places of learning as well as reflection, contemplation and retreat. More specifically, they represented a commitment to faith and a set of ideological (and theological) principles that defined their existence and that resulted from a search for meaning and deep understanding of how Christians should be in their world.

Though self-selected, the monastery models an alternative lifestyle and set of values to the larger society and culture. Among other things, the monastery implied that faith is both developed and expressed in the context of community. Faith does not happen alone. The monastery, then, offers a particular expression of God's Kingdom in the world; a kind of social, intellectual and religious center for those of the surrounding city and countryside. As Henri Nouwen, referring to his experience among the Trappists, puts it, "In so far as the monastery is the place where the presence of God in the world is most explicitly manifest and brought to consciousness, it is indeed the center of the world."[26]

But the monastery could not exist in isolation. Though the world and the flesh were considered distractions, the monastic orders had to come to terms with the larger world either as a place to carry out the mandates of service to God or simply in the interests of physical survival. To remain viable required developing some kind of relationships and interchange with the larger world outside. A kind of marketplace, both figurative and real, grew up outside the monastery walls where members of the monastic community engaged in a commerce of goods and ideas with those from the outside. The marketplace became quite literally the "locus of *praxis,*" the place where the pragmatic, survival-oriented, everyday world outside was engaged by the pious, idealistic, reflective one of the monastery.

As a metaphor, the relationship between monastery and the marketplace illustrates something of the relation between the Christian liberal arts college and "real world" professions such as education, law, medicine or business. Like the monastery, the Christian liberal arts college represents a particular expression of religious order and community. It is a place of contemplation, of faith and even of spiritual retreat. Its ideological and theological core defines the essence of its existence. The word "college" itself derives from the Latin *collegium* — a community of peers committed to a common enterprise and to each other. Like the monastery, the college offers a community and a center to the larger world; an alternative style of living and thinking that are based on foundational premises and commonly held values. The Christian college offers an alternative set of values to those of the dominant culture. But, like its medieval counterpart, the Christian-college-as-monastery needs to enter into the commerce of the marketplace if it is to remain ideologically (and even physically) viable. To do so is, as Richard A. Yoder recently suggested, to "take to the road," engaging God's creation and people in their own context and hearing their stories.[27] Such "commerce" is one in which the world outside tests and validates or repudiates the ideas and the practice offered from within. Indeed, it offers a context for mutual validation: the marketplace as a test of monastic idealism and ideology, and the monastery as a center from which to challenge the assumptions and the values that prevail in the marketplace. The monastery enters the marketplace because it must make concrete the abstractions that constitute their daily stock in trade. By the same token, without the ideals of community, order, ethics and meaning offered by the monastic center the world outside dissolves into selfishness, chaos and incoherence. The marketplace then becomes a venue for *praxis,* a place where ideology and idealism interface with pragmatism and "real world" application.

The monastic metaphor as a way of characterizing the Fresno Pacific College story suggests a series of outwardly expanding circles as the college moved from its more insular Bible institute beginnings to the more pure liberal arts focus and then still further to the present-day graduate level professional programs. The metaphor suggests a progressive opening of doors in the monastic walls that facilitates ease of movement in and out. Though not without some dis-ease, the college has moved toward a notion of the world "outside" as a sphere for exchange and influence. To do professional preparation programs, then, was to offer a special point of interface between monastery and marketplace.

The metaphor brings with it, in the concept of "profession," a notion of a common ground that contains both theory and practice; both a body of knowledge and its application. Knowledge of both theory and context enables the expert analysis and selective application that characterizes the professional level of practice. Thus even the professional person functions in the marketplace while remaining rooted in a kind of community, ideology and idealism coming out of the "monastery."

This notion implies that in order to do professional programs, Christian college faculty must seek appreciation—if not necessarily personal affinity—for both worlds: the cloister and the marketplace. This seems very much like the call by Lynn Curry and others for both academics and professionals to engage in the "scholarship of practice." Such a conception de-emphasizes the distinction between "scholars" and "professionals."[28] It requires both to work at integration; to understand both practice and reflection as necessary parts of a synergistic whole. This is not to say that some within academe may not find their gifts best exercised in the more contemplative world of the monastic tradition. Others, similarly, may find their primary place in direct engagement with the noise and bustle of the marketplace. Probably only a small number will feel completely at home within both worlds. To do so requires a kind of "bilingualism," even "biculturalism" that is not easy to attain or maintain. Yet it seems clear that in order to do professional or higher level academic program with integrity, all members of the Christian college community must participate deeply in a common ideology that grows out of the shared reflection and order of the monastery even as they engage the chaos and confusion of the world outside.

To do both liberal arts and professional education within a Christian college is to embrace a dialectic; working out an articulation between core ideology and program without assuming the primacy of one over the other. At best, such a core and its programmatic expression offer validation to each other: a kind of reciprocal "salting and lighting" of both marketplace and monastery.

The power of the Fresno Pacific Idea lies in its ability to offer a theological and moral community and center from which to view and to engage the world and from which to carry out a mandate to help "bring in the Kingdom." The "Idea" provides a distinctive platform from which to critique the prevailing culture of professional practice; bringing to that world the ethos and ethics of God's kingdom. In its focus on the foundationality of Christ, the holism of the liberal arts and the role of community, the Idea offers a center fashioned, finally, around a view of Truth that is paradoxically both propositional and incarnational; a view that holds that Truth can only be known by the integration of thinking and acting, of being and doing.

NOTES

1. Joel Wiebe, *Remembering . . . Reaching: A Vision of Service: A Fifty Year History of Fresno Pacific College* (Fresno: Fresno Pacific College, 1994), chap. 1.

2. See, for example, Clara Lovett, "To Affect Intimately the Lives of the People: American Professors and Their Society," *Change* 25 (July/August 1993): 26-37; or Stanley Hauerwas, *Christian Existence Today: Essays on Church, World and Living in Between* (Durham, N.C.: The Labyrinth Press, 1988). See particularly his chapter "How Universities Contribute to the Corruption of Youth," 237-252.

3. Delbert Wiens, "Rethinking FPC," A paper presented to the Fresno Pacific College Faculty Caucus, 18 April 1985, Records of Fresno Pacific College, Center for Mennonite Brethren Studies, Fresno, Calif. (Hereafter FPC Records).

4. Silas Bartsch, interview with author, 30 October 1992.

5. Delbert Wiens, "Rethinking FPC."

6. Bartsch, interview.

7. John Redekop, Interview with author, 6 February 1993.

8. Pacific Bible Institute Catalog, 1945-1946, 8.

9. Delbert Wiens, "Prolegomenon," Papers of Delbert Wiens, Center for Mennonite Brethren Studies, Fresno, Calif.

10. Minutes, Pacific College Corporation Board of Directors Records, 26-28 October 1965, Records of the Board of Education of the United States Mennonite Brethren Church, Center for Mennonite Brethren Studies, Fresno, Calif. (Hereafter Board of Education Records).

11. Faculty Meeting minutes, 22 May 1967, FPC Records.

12. See, for example, Harold S. Bender, "The Anabaptist Vision," *Church History* 13 (April 1944): 3-28; Guy F. Hershberger, *War, Peace and Nonresistance* (Scottdale, Pa.: Herald Press, 1944); Guy F. Hershberger, ed., *The Recovery of the Anabaptist Vision: A Sixtieth Anniversary Tribute to Harold S. Bender* (Scottdale, Pa.: Herald Press, 1957).

13. Joel Wiebe, *Remembering*, 102.

14. Joel Wiebe, Interview with author, November 1993.

15. "The Pacific College Graduate Program," document in possession of author.

16. "Fresno Pacific College Information Bulletin: Program Leading to the Degree Master of Arts in Education: Administrative Services," September 1977, Fresno Pacific College Records.

17. Fresno Pacific College Graduate Council Minutes, 18 January 1984, Fresno Pacific College Records.

18. Ibid.

19. "Fresno Pacific College In-service Program Mission Statement," Board of Trustees Academic Commission minutes, 23 April 1988, Fresno Pacific College Records.

20. Ibid.

21. Of course, the liberal arts focus of Fresno Pacific was probably never completely pure. As early as 1949 a program was outlined that was intended to lead to a teaching credential (See Joel Wiebe, *Remembering*, 48). A 1983 memorandum from then-dean Robert Enns to the Academic Commission of the Board noted, further, that the college has increased faculty FTE in "professional and vocational" areas as a response to "the interests of prospective students, and Board" without "weakening the liberal arts orientation of the college.(Robert Enns, Report to the Academic Commission: Board of Trustee's Minutes, 18 June 1983, Fresno Pacific College Records.

22. Lovett, "To Affect Intimately," 31.

23. Ibid., 31.

24. Ibid., 33.

25. Delbert Wiens, "Rethinking FPC," 3.

26. Henri J. Nouwen, *The Genesee Diary: Report from a Trappist Monastery,* (Garden City, N.Y.: Image Books, 1981), 170.

27. Richard A. Yoder and Carolyn Yoder, "Questions On the Road," *Crossroads* 75 (Winter 1994): 4-9.

28. Lynn Curry, et al., *Educating Professionals: Responding to New Expectations for Competence and Accountability* (San Francisco: Jossey-Bass, 1993).

Epilogue

The Fresno Pacific College Idea is now a nearly thirty-year effort to create a distinctive Christian liberal arts college. In many ways the story is a very successful one. In the past years the college has gained national recognition. In the early 1990s U. S. *News and World Report* ranked it as among the "up and coming" or "best" small colleges in the West. Its dramatic growth during the last decade, the achievements of its graduates, and its increasing prominence in the San Joaquin Valley are testimonials to a successful college.

This successful history, as these essays suggest, is also a story of paradox and ambiguity. It contains the essential dialectic of theory and praxis — the difficulty of giving ideas institutional forms, or to use biblical language, of incarnating them. The mind can outrun the constraints of student needs, accrediting agency criteria and the auditors' insistence on paying the bills in a timely fashion. Robert Enns invokes the stories of Brandeis, Wheaton and Guilford seeking to hold together commitments that sometimes pull in opposite directions. These essays suggest the differing ways in which FPC has tried to hold together sometimes conflicting ideas — liberal arts and professional education; Mennonite particularity and evangelical ecumenicity; a supporting denomination with an immigrant past and a strong sense of ethno-religious boundaries and ethnic inclusiveness; a strong sense of community and cultural diversity. Straddling those differing ideals and realities is not peculiar to Fresno Pacific College. The building of national and international cultures during the past century has brought the same pressures to many institutions and communities.

The college's self-conscious adoption, in the early 1980s, of a strategy to "Broaden the Base" only multiplied the diversity of students, faculty and institutional supporters. If defined in numerical terms, that strategy has certainly been successful. The decade since 1985 in many ways paralleled the explosive growth of the 1960s. In addition to dramatic enrollment growth, the physical appearance of the campus changed significantly through the addition of three new buildings. During the past decade the college has also undergone a process of maturation. In so doing it became more things to more people. It serves more diverse publics than at any other time in its history. As that happens the centripetal forces can easily overwhelm the centrifugal restraints.

At one level, the "Broadening" transition did exactly that, but at another level it has not. Concurrent with the writing of these essays has been a faculty/administrative process of reflection and revision of the Fresno Pacific College Idea. The third form of the idea (following the 1966 and 1982 editions) was formally ratified by the college's Board of Trustees in January 1995. Unlike the 1982 revision, the impetus for which came from the Board of Trustees, this one came from internal pressures. The significant influx of both new faculty and administrators in the decade following 1985 called for a sustained dialogue about institutional mission and identity.

The 1982 revision diminished the distinctive elements and pushed the college toward becoming a more generic evangelical college. This revision articulated a more distinctive mission statement. A committee composed of John Yoder (Graduate Dean) and Rod Janzen (faculty), together with trustees Winnie Bartel and Patrick Evans, held campus-wide hearings and submitted a revised document for community discussion and consensus-building. With Yoder and Janzen as the principal authors, the document embraced the enlarged diversity of the campus. More than previous versions of the Idea, it offered an understanding of Christian faith as transcending and including cultural, racial, ethnic and ideological partialities. All have room in a community seeking to establish a foretaste of the inclusiveness of the Kingdom of God. Simultaneously, this revision, more than the 1982 version, emphasized the prophetic function of a college that stands in the Anabaptist-Mennonite tradition. Authentic knowledge and understanding need to be transformative. They not only "illuminate darkness with light and dispel ignorance with wisdom," as the document suggests, but they also "contribute to developing a vision for wholeness, justice and reconciliation."

The revisioning of the document was clearly part of a larger dialectic. Precisely as Fresno Pacific College became more ecumenical and diverse it needed to identify its particularity. As the boundaries became more permeable, it was incumbent again to rearticulate the center. As the college gained a greater measure of success and solidity it had a greater freedom again to dream of being a distinctive college. After the college had proven itself as evangelical, it had a new opportunity again to articulate its Anabaptism.

For a long time the West's prevailing understanding of modernity was that the plurality of the past would of necessity give way to a more uniform future. Global integration would inevitably result in greater sameness. During the past fifty years it has been easy for various commentators to write of a coming world unity. In the United States throughout much of the twentieth century we utilized the image of the "melting pot" to visualize the kind of society that we were building. The melting pot metaphor assumed that each particular group contributed some distinguishing ingredient to the new American culture that was being built, but that the ingredient only flavored it rather than remaining distinctive or autonomous. In Christian higher education the non-denominational college represented the search for a homogenous Christian faith and presence in the world.

More recently we have come to understand that the American future is a pluralist one rather than an integrative one. We are a nation of diverse races, cultures, ethnicities and denominations. Each contributes to the richness of the larger culture. Denominations, which can be interpreted as the failure of the church, can also be seen as the smaller incarnations of the God we worship, who transcends any particular form. Colleges that nurture distinctive theological ideas also contribute to the richness and pluralism of American higher education. To the degree that Fresno Pacific College works at the incarnation of the Fresno Pacific College Idea it also makes such a contribution.

Appendix

The Evolution of the
Fresno Pacific College Idea

Original edition (1966)

Fresno Pacific College is a deliberate and continuous attempt to realize a certain idea through theory and experience. The components of this idea are described in the following concepts:

Fresno Pacific College is a Christian College

The college accepts as the ultimate authority for life God's self-disclosure of himself to man in Jesus Christ and in the record of Scripture. This affirmation gives purpose, meaning, and unity to knowledge and education. Because the college believes in the unity of all knowledge under God, it sees no ultimate contradiction between the truth of revelation and of scholarly investigation. It therefore enjoys both the freedom of inquiry and the freedom of commitment.

As a college committed to Christian revelation, Fresno Pacific seeks to educate the whole person, nurturing every phase of man's free and creative development—spiritually, morally, intellectually, culturally, and physically.

Fresno Pacific College is a Community

The college strives to be a community where interpersonal relations play a vital role in the process of education. The college believes that disengagement from people is an evasion of the real task of education. It intends rather to foster an open, free, honest, and creative interrelationship among all members of the community.

While the college is not interested in forcing the student to subscribe to the teacher's point of view, it intends the teacher to serve as a model for the student through his own life and as a catalyst for the student's thinking through the exposition and defense of his own position on various issues. The college assumes that learning involves interaction between people and ideas and encourages learning that will result in worthwhile and intelligent commitments.

The college seeks to encourage the acceptance of every person as an individual. The college believes that everyone has individuality, value, equality, and purpose. It therefore seeks to give each member of the college community the personal courage to cope with the normal anxieties of the college learning experience and to accept new insights and new truths. It seeks through interpersonal relationships to enable each person to learn, to change, and to make new and meaningful commitments.

Therefore, the college is a resident community. It believes that the instruction of the classroom is only one aspect of learning. The continuous interaction which the life and study of the whole campus provides may be as significant as the instruction of the classroom. It is the involvement of the individual in the total community of the college that forms and modifies the ideals of the community members.

Because the college believes that it is better for men and women to meet each other daily in such a community, and in a variety of activities and situations, Fresno Pacific is a coeducational community. It believes that the estimates of one another based upon natural and varied interrelationships are likely to be more realistic, and the consequent life adjustments more soundly based.

The college believes that authentic community is found as man relates to God through faith. It therefore hopes that the members of the community are, or will become, believers in Jesus Christ who seek for a fuller understanding and experience of Him through study, sharing, meditation, prayer, and worship. It will not, however, discriminate against students who cannot freely and honestly make such a commitment.

Fresno Pacific College is a Liberal Arts College

The objective of the college is to provide a progression of experiences leading the student: (1) to a wholeness of personality characterized by personal understanding and freedom of action, (2) to a more perceptive and creative relationship with God and the world, (3) to an understanding of the interrelationship of knowledge and the methodologies unique to the areas of knowledge, and (4) to the point where he can independently and capably manage knowledge.

It is held that exposure to that liberal arts tradition which has sought to understand God, man, and the world through the disciplines of theology, philosophy, mathematics, the natural and physical sciences, the social sciences, and the fine and communicative arts is most relevant in providing the range of experiences leading to the achievement of this objective.

Training for effectiveness in the professions is considered to be an aspect of the educational program at Fresno Pacific. But, highly technical, professional training apart from the liberal arts tradition is inconsistent with the basic objectives of the institution. Consistent with the primary focus of the college, students in a professional course of training will always be required to have a significant concentration of work in the liberal arts tradition.

Fresno Pacific College is an Experimental College

The college seeks to add to existing knowledge in improved forms. Teachers at Fresno Pacific are encouraged to engage in original research in their respective disciplines as long as such research does not detract from their effectiveness as teachers. The college is continuously searching for better ways to prepare its students for meaningful roles in society, the professions, the family, and the church.

Fresno Pacific College is an Anabaptist-Mennonite College

Fresno Pacific is a Mennonite Brethren educational institution. As a college in the Anabaptist-Mennonite tradition, the college seeks to recapture the faith and life of the early Christian church, placing central emphasis upon the Lordship of Jesus Christ for the totality of life, the authority of the Scriptures for all matters of faith and ethics, the Christian life as a life of discipleship, the Christian church as a fellowship of redeemed people, the voluntary nature of faith and the freedom of conscience, and the active application of love to the whole of life, including the promotion of peace and nonresistance, missions, relief, mutual aid, and voluntary service.

The college, as an institution of the church, seeks to relate to the church through conversation and leadership. It intends to educate people who will understand the church and provide perceptive and creative leadership in the church.

Fresno Pacific College is a Non-Sectarian College

Religious discrimination of a narrow sectarian nature is not imposed in the admissions policy of the college. Anyone wanting a Christian education is invited to join Fresno Pacific in a quest for meaning and wholeness of life.

Fresno Pacific College is a Prophetic College

The college views itself as a center of independent critique of all of man's endeavors. It is not simply an institution that transmits the values of the culture in which it exists. It purposes to serve as the conscience of society and the church rather than become a tool of any institution or idealism.

The Fresno Pacific idea is only a partially realized idea. But it is the idea that gives Fresno Pacific reason for existence, courage for growth, and stimulus for adventure.

Revised edition (1982)

The Fresno Pacific College Idea is a guide for the future; it is also a process of the present and an outgrowth of the past.

As the college seeks to accomplish its educational mission, it affirms the significance of knowledge which leads to wisdom, encourages virtue, establishes harmony, and creates balance and perspective.

As a Christian liberal arts college, Fresno Pacific College is an integral part of the mission of the church. Through the liberal arts, the college provides knowledge and experience which lead toward a more perceptive and creative relationship with God, humanity, and the world. On this foundation of Christian perspectives and liberal arts education, the college provides preparation for service to church and society through vocational and professional development. The college is a community in which interpersonal relationships play a vital role in the process of education.

Fresno Pacific College is a Christian College

As a Christian college, Fresno Pacific College considers a primary goal to be the integration of faith and learning. In pursuing this goal it accepts the unity of all knowledge under God; it perceives no ultimate contradiction between the truth of revelation and of scholarly investigation.

With others in the Believers' Church tradition the college encourages voluntary acknowledgement of the sovereignty of God and the triumph of his kingdom, the presence of his Spirit in the life of the church, and the lordship of Jesus Christ over all of life.

As an extension of the educational mission of the Mennonite Brethren Church, the college affirms the authority of Scripture over all matters of faith and life; the church as a community of redeemed people; the life of discipleship which leads to holiness, witness, and service; the call to serve Christ by proclaiming the Gospel, ministering to human need, and alleviating suffering; the practice of reconciliation and love in settings of violence, oppression, and injustice; and the development of spiritual maturity through the disciplines of prayer, study and meditation.

Believing that the Gospel transcends the limitations of all cultures and ideologies, the college encourages persons to serve throughout the world as compassionate Christian disciples and constructive members of society.

Fresno Pacific College Is a Liberal Arts College

As a liberal arts college, Fresno Pacific College provides an education which leads to an examined understanding of God, humanity, and the world through the disciplines of theology, philosophy, the humanities, and the social and natural sciences.

Education is a comprehensive process; the college is concerned with the whole person and seeks to nurture every phase of development — spiritual, moral, intellectual, cultural, social, physical.

Education includes a training process; preparing persons for leadership, ministry, and service in a variety of vocations and professions is an important aspect of education. However, the college considers vocational preparation to be more than the acquisition of information and skills; it is also the formation of values which enrich the meaning and enhance the quality of work. Professional programs therefore emphasize the integration of Christian faith and the liberal arts with career development.

Education is a life-long process in which analytical thinking and creative reflection lead to spiritual, personal, and professional maturity. The college therefore extends its educational boundaries to include older as well as younger adults in a variety of settings; its mission includes post-baccalaureate programs which provide for personal enrichment and professional growth. It invites persons from various cultural, national, ethnic, and religious settings and backgrounds to participate in the educational experience.

Fresno Pacific College is a Community

As an educational community, Fresno Pacific College recognizes the value of interpersonal relationships in the process of education. It assumes that learning is the result of interaction between people and ideas; as individuals are more responsible with, and accountable to, one another, they are more able to understand themselves and to make perceptive commitments to God, the church, and the world. While the college affirms that community which is formed as its members relate to God, it does not discriminate against those who cannot freely and honestly make such a commitment.

The college accepts each member as a unique person with purpose and value. It seeks to provide settings in which each individual can gain new insights and experiences, develop new relationships, and make meaningful commitments.

While acknowledging and respecting individual differences, the college affirms the Believers' Church expression of community as a body which transcends individualism as well as those cultural, national, and ethnic boundaries which may separate and alienate. Since involvement in mutual worship, study, work, and play strengthens the life of both the individual and the community, residence on campus is encouraged as a means of experiencing the richness of this community.

The college fulfills its mission as it incorporates faculty who participate in church and society as role models in relating Christian faith to matters of thought and action; students who share a mutual respect for educational goals and community standards; staff who are committed to enhancing the quality of the educational experience; and a board which encourages understanding and support for the mission of the college.

Revised edition (1995)

The Fresno Pacific College Idea reflects the college's interpretation of what it means to be a community of learners committed to a distinctive vision of Christian higher education. The Idea serves as a center for reflection and action and as a guide for forming a vision of the future. Rooted in the past and continuously re-shaped by the present, the Idea provides a foundation for the college's understanding of itself and of the mission to which it is called.

In pursuing this mission, the college affirms the significance of knowledge which is a foundation for wisdom and virtue. As a Christian liberal arts community, Fresno Pacific College is an integral part of the mission of the church. From this Christian and liberal arts center the college seeks to engage members of its community in a collaborative search for knowledge and experience which lead toward a perceptive and creative relationship with God, humanity, and the natural world. On this foundation, the college seeks to build and to extend the Kingdom of God by enabling persons to serve church and society.

The Fresno Pacific College Idea articulates the college's primary identity, its vision of community, and its relation to the larger world. The parts of the Idea are not mutually exclusive. but complementary. Together, they form an organic whole.

Fresno Pacific College is a Christian College

Fresno Pacific College seeks to be a collegium centered upon Christ and His church. It is committed to the ideals of God's Kingdom and to the perspective of the liberal arts in which integration of faith, learning, and action is a primary goal.

With others in the Anabaptist-Mennonite and Believers Church tradition, the college encourages voluntary acknowledgment of the sovereignty of God, of the triumph of God's Kingdom, of the presence of God's Spirit in the life of the church, and of the Lordship of Christ in all of life.

As an extension of the educational mission of the Mennonite Brethren Church, the college affirms the authority of the Bible over all matters of faith and life; the church as a community of redeemed people; a life of discipleship leading to holiness, witness, and service; the call to serve Jesus by ministering to human need and alleviating suffering; the practice of reconciliation and love in settings of violence, oppression, and injustice; and the development of spiritual maturity through disciplines such as prayer, study and meditation.

All authentic knowledge and experience are unified under God. All aspects of reality are understood to be parts of a larger whole. There is no contradiction then between the truth of revelation, of scholarly investigation, and of action. The college encourages members of the Fresno Pacific community toward a reflective and critical perspective on the nature of humanity and its relation to the world. Thus the liberal arts enlarge the foundation for life-long learning and for advanced study in a discipline or profession. The college affirms that wisdom grows out of commitment to Christian faith and to the integrative perspective of the liberal arts. Both are essential to developing a wholistic view of God, self, and the world.

Since education is understood to be a life-long process, the college programs include a variety of academic and professional undergraduate, graduate, and non-degree programs. Each program builds on the integrative foundation of the liberal arts, encouraging thoughtful reflection on those beliefs and values that contribute to personal and societal wholeness. The intersection of Christian belief, the liberal arts, and an ethic of service provide an educational perspective that leads to an examined understanding of God, self, and the world, uniting theory with practice.

Fresno Pacific College is a Community of Learners

Fresno Pacific College recognizes the importance of the interpersonal dimension of the learning process. The college believes that community grows out of common commitments, and that learning is the result of interaction between persons, ideas and experience. Thus the college seeks to provide settings in which individuals can achieve such interaction within a community committed to learning and service. It believes that as individuals become more responsible with, and accountable to, one another, they are better able to understand themselves and to make thoughtful commitments to God, the church, and the world

The college seeks to accept each member of the community as unique, with purpose and value. Ethnic and religious identity is affirmed as a basis for respectful pluralism. While acknowledging individual differences, the college also holds to the Believers Church expression of community as a body which transcends individualism and those cultural, national, and ethnic boundaries which separate and alienate.

Believing that the Gospel transcends the limitations of all cultures and ideologies and that inclusiveness enriches community, Fresno Pacific College welcomes those of different cultural, national, ethnic, and religious backgrounds to participate in its educational experience. The college invites those from other church traditions, both as faculty and students, to enter into dialogue and faithful practice with those in the Anabaptist and Believers Church tradition in following Christ and in sharing the college's mission. In keeping with its voluntaristic church tradition, the college affirms the community formed as individuals relate to God and does not discriminate against students who cannot freely and honestly make such a commitment. The college encourages persons to serve across cultures and throughout the world as compassionate disciples of Christ and as constructive members of society.

The college believes that knowledge and understanding are formed in community; that learning takes place through dialogue and discourse between people who have different experiences and perspectives, and that such wisdom begins with humility. These understandings join teachers and students as partners in a mutual search for truth and wholeness.

The college's belief in community expresses itself in patterns of leadership and governance that are servant oriented and participatory and which lead toward consensual decision making.

The college seeks to carry out its educational mission through faculty, students, staff and board who participate in church and society, share a mutual respect for educational goals and community standards and are committed to enhancing the quality of the educational experience for all its members.

Fresno Pacific College is Prophetic

Fresno Pacific College believes that to be prophetic is to serve the church and society by engaging in dialogue with and critique of contemporary culture and practice. The college encourages informed reflection on personal, institutional and societal values which contribute to developing a vision for wholeness, justice and reconciliation. It offers leadership to the church and the world by enabling persons to extend perceptive, creative, and skillful responses to current issues; to illuminate darkness with light and dispel ignorance with wisdom and understanding. It seeks to bring an integrative, Christian ethic and perspective to present day thought and experience and to a common search for the better way.

Fresno Pacific College understands learning to be a journey; a journey of exploration, reflection and transformation; a journey toward deepened meaning and faith growing out of creative encounter with Christ and the world. The college believes that such learning may be nurtured through many different modalities and in many different settings and that it should be encouraged to continue throughout life. Thus the college values imaginative, experimental and innovative ways of engaging students and faculty in the process of learning even as it seeks to remain faithful to its core values and identity.

Fresno Pacific College is a deliberate and continuing attempt to realize the vision expressed in the Fresno Pacific College Idea. The Idea gives the college reason for existence, courage for growth, and stimulus for adventure.

Contributors

ROBERT ENNS
Professor of Sociology. Joined the faculty in 1970. From 1981 to 1985 was Dean of the College.

WILFRED MARTENS
Professor of English. Joined the faculty in 1965. For many years has been Chair of the English Department or Chair of the Humanities Division.

DALTON REIMER
Undergraduate Dean, Professor of Communication, Co-Director of the Center for Conflict Studies and Peacemaking. Joined the faculty in 1960. From 1971 to 1981 was Dean of the College.

PAUL TOEWS
Professor of History, Director of the Center for Mennonite Brethren Studies. Joined the faculty in 1967.

ARTHUR WIEBE
President Emeritus and Professor of Mathematics Education Emeritus. Director of the AIMS Foundation, a research and educational agency affiliated with the College. Joined the faculty in 1960. From 1960 to 1975 was President of the College.

DELBERT WIENS
Professor of Humanities, Philosophy and History. Joined the faculty in 1969.

JOHN YODER
Dean of Graduate Studies, Professor of Education. Joined the faculty in 1991.

DATE DUE

1/2/97			
12-20-96			

GAYLORD   PRINTED IN U.S.A